TOWARDS
MULTIPLE PERSPECTIVES
ON LITERACY

FIFTY-NINTH YEARBOOK
OF THE
CLAREMONT READING CONFERENCE

Sponsored by
The Claremont Graduate School

Edited By

PHILIP H. DREYER

Continuing Conference Theme:

READING, THE PROCESS OF CREATING
MEANING FOR SENSED STIMULI

Price $20.00

Back issues of the Claremont Reading Conference are available from
two sources. Volumes still in print may be ordered from the following
address: Claremont Reading Conference Yearbook, Harper 200,
Claremont Graduate School, Claremont, California 91711-6160. Write
for information concerning books in print and special price list. All
past Yearbooks are available through University Microfilms, 300 Zeeb
Road, Ann Arbor, Michigan 48103.

© 1995 by The Claremont Reading Conference

ISBN #0-941742-15-6

Published by The Claremont Reading Conference
Institute for Developmental Studies
The Claremont Graduate School, Claremont, California 91711-6160

TABLE OF CONTENTS

iii

Acknowledgments

Planning for the Claremont Reading Conference of 1995 began in the summer of 1994 with the help of Michele Foster, Abbie Prentice, Thomas Caughron, Jan Malin, Doty Hale, Sally Thomas, Velma Sablan, Caroline Angus, Evelyn Weisman, and Sue Abel. This group chose the conference theme and nominated keynote speakers. As the conference unfolded, they gave unstintingly of their wisdom, energy, and vast experience. The coordinator of the Conference was Joe Wakelee-Lynch who mastered the details of room arrangements, programs, correspondence, and the many ambiguities of such an event with calm and competence.

The preparation of this Yearbook was done by Teresa Wilborn and Ethel Rogers of The Claremont Graduate School Center for Educational Studies, while the layout and printing were coordinated by Martha Estus of the CGS Public Affairs Office. Joe Wakelee-Lynch kept the mailing lists straight and organized the distribution of yearbooks.

Special thanks also go to the faculty in The Center for Educational Studies of The Claremont Graduate School, especially Michele Foster, Mary Poplin, and David Drew, whose creativity and support are essential to the continued success of the Conference.

Philip H. Dreyer
Reading Conference Director
Yearbook Editor

Introduction to the 59th Yearbook

During its long tenure, the Claremont Reading Conference has consistently focused on the theme that "reading is making meaning from sensed stimuli." Over the years this general definition, with its focus on the natural process of language development in children and upon children's experiences with stories in all forms, has evolved into what is now called the "whole language" approach to literacy. In this view reading is not a subject to be taught but a description of the activities that people engage in when they come to understand the world around them. For example, we "read" the sky to understand the weather and we "read" the smells in our kitchen to know what's for dinner, just as we "read" the newspaper or a novel. Reading is an active process, one which differs from person to person and from event to event.

For many years this view of reading was out of favor with the professional education community who create materials for our public schools. They preferred to view reading as a collection of discrete activities, such as letter recognition and sight/sound correspondences, which can be taught incrementally in small steps, leading from the basics of sounding out alphabet letters to word recognition and then to the deciphering of sentences. Whole language approaches were seen in this period as an alternative theory of reading which did not lend itself well to the needs of professional curriculum designers, book publishers, and lesson planners. This set of attitudes changed in the late 1980's, however, when growing dissatisfaction with the reading test scores of elementary school children led to a major reconsideration of reading instruction and language arts curriculum. The sense that something was wrong with the reading curriculum led to a search for alternatives, and the whole language approach was rediscovered and brought forward by policy makers as a possible solution to the problem of low reading test scores. A number of states, such as California, adopted the whole language approach for the language arts curriculum, thrusting whole language into the spotlight of educational reform.

The result of the decision by states like California to adopt whole language as the core of its language arts curriculum is that whole language has suddenly become both a political and a commercial issue. Politically, whole language is now seen as a unitary set of instructional methods and classroom activities which can be subjected to psychometric evaluation and statistical analysis. The political issue, in short, is not literacy but test scores, and the political criterion is brutally pragmatic--raise test scores or else. Commercially, whole language has become grist for the publishers' mill, and the people who produced basal readers for generations apply their experience to children's literature. Inexpensive, large print, single color editions of children's literature "classics" have been printed for use by entire classes, and these come complete with teacher's guide, suggested class activities, and test questions. Any similarity between these materials and the original stories is strictly coincidental. But like the political criterion for success, the commercial drive for economic profit is brutally practical.

What is lost in this blaze of educational reform is the nature of the educational objective itself—literacy. Literacy involves the ability of people to derive meaning from the world around them, especially the media—books, newspapers, computers, television, and live performances, among others. How individuals do this—how they "read" something and "comprehend" it—is a complex process which can be encouraged, modeled, and reinforced, but not "taught" in a simplistic, mechanistic way. It is a process which is "learned" but not "taught." The tendency of the leaders of the current wave of educational reform is to abandon this objective in favor of "accountability," namely high test scores and large economic profits for publishers. Yet, it is important to keep in mind that high test scores do not necessarily mean that children are literate, and high publisher profits do not necessarily mean that children are having useful experiences in schools.

Using the bottom line approach of test scores and profits, whole language will probably be deemed a "failure" by current educational reformers, because it does not address the kinds of issues traditional tests usually measure and traditional school publishers usually create. What the whole language approach does is to take a multifaceted approach to the larger educational goal of literacy. It focuses on what children know and can understand, not how they memorize letter sounds or speak printed sentences. It brings together reading and writing as two aspects of the same issue, encouraging children to be authors and creators, not just readers and consumers. And it relies upon the close interaction of young inexperienced readers with older, more competent readers and story tellers who serve as models and supporters.

Whether these lessons about whole language reading theory can be absorbed and put to good use before the current wave of political educational reform is deemed a failure appears doubtful at this time. Yet, the search for "meaning" will go on and the effort to better understand the process of reading in all its forms will continue to inspire the Claremont Reading Conference and the people who make this volume possible. The articles in this volume were created from presentations at the 62nd annual Claremont Reading Conference, which was held on the campuses of the Claremont Colleges March 17 and 18, 1995.

The papers presented here are not grouped in any particular order and do not represent a particular point of view. Instead, they represent the kind of variety and energy which surrounds the issues of reading, writing, and literacy in its broadest sense. Our hope in this volume is to capture the quality of the conference and to share these ideas with a wider audience.

Philip H. Dreyer, Ph. D.
Professor of Education

RELEARNING THE ALPHABET: MY NEW APPRECIATION OF LITERACY

A Slide Presentation*

Dianne Johnson-Feelings

When I began reflecting on the significance of literacy in my personal experience, I realized that I think about "literacy" every day. In fact, I used to be a literacy volunteer, an experience that turned out to be a very negative one for me when my student fired me. The worst part of the situation was that I never found out why she discontinued our partnership. I have various hunches. To begin with, our lives were very different. She worked hard in a factory every day of the week. I had only to look at her hands to know that. At night and on weekends she studied cosmetology. She wanted to get her GED so that she could be an example for her sons. I imagine that to her, about the same age as myself, I seemed like a spoiled college girl. Her husband, who regularly sabotaged our phone messages, didn't care who I was, but cared only that his wife did not have a degree while he did not.

When I think back on that scenario, I can't help but recall *The Narrative of the Life of Frederick Douglass*, a book that I teach often in my African American literature courses. I think about the meanings of literacy to slaves and wonder whether or

---

*The text may seem disjointed at points, because in this form it is disconnected from the visual portion of the text and lacks the asides I made about various slides and books.

not African American young people today would be inspired simply by knowing that it was once against the law of the land for an African to be able to read or write; whether or not they would see their own literacy, today, as a means of empowerment.

My more immediate task is to get my college students to think about the significance of literacy. Too many of them think that they are literate because they know how to read and to write. They don't realize that they are not literate if they cannot read and write **effectively**, if they can't communicate **clearly**. I don't like writing on papers "I know what you're trying to say." College students should be able to say precisely what they want to say. At the very least, they could use the spell-checker on their computers. Beyond that, they must recognize that there are reasons for rules of grammar and spelling; rules that have to do with clarity. If we are not clear, eventually all communication will break down. Students need to be savvy enough to realize that mastery of the English language relates, in a big way, to their status in this society.

As a native of South Carolina, as an African American, and as a person who is interested in language, I have a particular interest in Gullah, the basis of Black English Vernacular, spoken on the South Carolina and Georgia sea islands. There's a lot to be said about Gullah. It is a language with its own grammar, that embodies a particular philosophy of time, that has its own rhythm. But the one thing I must say to speakers of Black English and other non-standard languages is that to be successful in this society they have to master standard English. Of course, I always stress that what they refer to as "proper" English is more appropriately called "standard" English. I stress that the ideal is to be a master of a whole continuum of speech choices. I try to teach respect for all forms of English while at the same time doing my job as an English professor.

But my job has many sides. While I teach students to communicate clearly in standard English, I also teach the appreciation of literature. And as you know, creative writers are not, by any stretch of the imagination, obliged to follow the rules of any language. When parents and teachers criticize Lucille Clifton's children's books for her use of Black English, she answers that she is not a grammar teacher but a poet (Johnson, 1990, p. 115). Getting students to read the poetry, as it were; getting them to read children's literature critically, is an important part of my job.

The students who understand this from the beginning of the course are those who understand literacy in its broadest sense—reading, writing, and being conversant in one's culture; the ability to decipher the signs that surround us and shape our lives. The students who understand this understand that there are several kinds of literacy in the world of children's literature. Certainly, there is the written word, without which there is no publishing industry. In addition, there is aural literacy—we first experience language through our sense of hearing. And that is how many people experience picture books. In addition to the elements of written literacy and sound literacy is visual literacy—when dealing with picture books, the reader must read the illustrations.

Finally, those of us who use books must read context. Children do no need to be concerned with the politics of the publishing industry. But **someone** must be concerned or the resulting scenarios can be disastrous.

I'm not a literacy professional in the same way as those of you who are reading teaching teachers, for example. So after sending in the title and description printed in your programs I decided to change my focus. I've decided that my contribution to this conference would be to talk about what I know best—African American children's literature and the context surrounding its existence. I'll be using slides primarily from picture books, but the larger points I hope to make are applicable to literature for any age groups. And please keep in mind that I won't be talking about how to use the literature in the classroom, but rather, why it should be in the classroom, and large considerations we should all be aware of regarding American culture, education, and the publishing industry. I won't address literacy directly, but it is always an underlying concern.

I want to begin with a verse called "Dedication" written by Jessie Fauset in *The Brownies' Book* magazine (January 1920, p. 32). What it is really about is the scarcity of books which speak in a special way to our children. It reads:

> To Children, who with eager look
> Scanned vainly library shelf and nook,
> For History or Song or Story
> That told of Colored Peoples' glory,—
> We dedicate THE BROWNIES' BOOK.

Most people are not aware that there is an entire world of books which can be called African American children's literature. Because we don't regularly see books with African American images in book stores, most of us assume that they don't exist. Of course, they don't exist in the numbers that they should; books written or illustrated by African Americans account for only about 2 percent of the few thousand titles published every year in this country. But even this small percentage amounts to more titles than most of us might assume; books that reflect and interpret every aspect of the lives and dreams of the diversity of people who make up Black America.

I date African American children's literature back to at least 1920, when W. E. B. DuBois and Augustus Dill published *The Brownies' Book*, which they described as "a little magazine for children—for all children, but especially for our, 'the Children of the Sun.'...It will be a thing of Joy and Beauty, dealing in Happiness, Laughter and Emulation, and designed especially for Kiddies from Six to Sixteen. It will seek to teach Universal Love and Brotherhood for all little folk—black and brown and yellow and white" (*The Crisis*, October 1919, pp. 285-286).

In the same year that *The Brownies' Book* began publication, *St. Nicholas*, the preeminent mainstream magazine, was publishing verses such as "Ten little nigger boys went out to dine. One choked his little self and then there were nine" (Elinor Sinnette, 1965, p. 134). At least in part, the stage was set for these kinds of images in magazines by the popularity of the 1898 book *The Story of Little Black Sambo*. Set in India, but with African-like characters, the British author essentially makes the statement that all people of color can be thrown into one huge group called "other." In response to these kinds of images, DuBois wrote this:

Heretofore the education of the Negro child has been too much in terms of white people.... All of the pictures he sees are of white people. Most of the books he reads are white. If he goes to a motion picture show, the same is true. If a Negro appears on the screen, he is usually a caricature or a clown. The result is that all of the Negro child's idealism, all his sense of the good, the great and the beautiful is associated with white people. The effect can be readily imagined. He unconsciously gets the impression that the Negro has little chance to be great, heroic or beautiful (*The Crisis*, 1919, pp. 285-286).

The editors also outlined objectives for the magazine which included the following:

1. to make them familiar with the history and achievements of the Negro race
2. to make them know that other colored children have grown into beautiful, useful and famous persons
3. to turn their little hurts and resentments into emulation, ambition, and love of their own homes and companions
4. to point out the best amusements and joys and worthwhile things of life
5. to inspire them to prepare for definite occupations and duties with a broad spirit of sacrifice (*The Crisis*, 1919, pp. 285-286).

One thing I want us to keep in mind is that Black writers and illustrators, of yesterday and today, all seem to have, to some degree, these same objectives in mind that DuBois outlined. Part of what this means is that African American children's literature has always considered Education one of its major goals— Education as opposed to entertainment alone. The obvious direction this goal of education points to is the writing and re-writing of history, in an effort to begin to address the miseducation that resulted from the one-sided and prejudiced histories taught in the classrooms and mythologies entrenched in popular thought. African American history begins, of course, in Africa. So we find a whole category of books about the Mother Continent.

Lucille Clifton's *All Us Come Cross the Water* (1973) is just one book that makes the connection between Africa and the rest of the African diaspora. And, in fact, one of the first books to do this was *Popo and Fifina: Children of Haiti* (1932) by celebrated writers Langston Hughes and Arna Bontemps. A young adult book that explores the same theme is Rosa Guy's *The Friends* (1973). These books ask the questions of what happens when the idea of sisterhood and brotherhood are tested in real life; what happens when Black Americans, Africans, and West Indians come together? These questions and the idea of the diaspora are crucial in the increasingly global village of which we are a part. Quite a few books are now available which introduce young readers both to Africa and to the Caribbean, as well as various African cultures within the United States.

More than a few books on the topic of slavery also exist, a topic which is important because the diaspora developed largely as a result of that institution. Notable among these is John O. Killens' *Great Gittin' Up Morning* (1972; set in South Carolina) and Jacob Lawrence's *Harriet and the Promised Land* (1968). One thing I want to bring to your attention is that throughout the history of African American children's literature, many of our most important artists, intellectuals, and writers have been engaged in its creation. In the white world, on the other hand, this has happened much less frequently. What this indicates to me, or what I choose to believe, is that African Americans have always recognized the importance of children's literature; that it is not assigned a peripheral, secondary status in relationship to other literature and art. For example, Faith Ringgold, known mostly for her quilt art, published *Tar Beach* several years ago. The main character, Cassie Louise Lightfoot, tells the reader that "Daddy took me to see the new union building he is working on.... But still he can't join the union because Grandpa wasn't a member."

There are two things I want to point out about this passage. First, African American children's literature is part of a larger body of literature that includes African American literature for adults—a literature that has political foundations; it is concerned with making some comment upon the society in which we live.

From my vantage point, it seems that African American children's literature does and must raise political questions because its very existence depends on a constellation of political forces and structures. This sometimes political nature of the texts is related, of course, to what can be called "the politics of the world of children's book publishing." And clearly, three quarters of a century after DuBois's statements, controversy still ensues around the question of authorship of literature about or for Black children. The identity of an author or illustrator is significant to a great extent with many texts. For example, a prolonged debate took place during the early eighties in response to *Jake and Honeybunch Go to Heaven* (1982), a retelling of a Black folktale. Written and illustrated by celebrated children's writer Margot Zemach, the book portrayed a man and his mule who are killed by a train, an important image in African American culture. They eventually enter a heaven presided over by a Black god who is dressed like Uncle Sam, inhabited by angels eating barbecue, and where Jake behaves like "a flying fool." According to Zemach, her purposed were "to write a book for black children, one that would preserve their folklore and that they could related to visually." Instead, what she produced was a book which was eventually banned or stored in closed reserves in many children's libraries because of its potential for perpetuating stereotypical images of African American people. At issue too is the phenomenon whereby often it is considered acceptable for members of a given group to denigrate or ridicule or poke fun at itself while it is unacceptable for nongroup members to do likewise. Mockery, good-natured as it might be, will not be accepted by Black Americans until there does exist, in fact, a balance of various kinds of Black images in literature.

One enormous issue which is, in some ways, at the very root of my comments, is the very definition of the term "African American children's literature." The term "children's literature" refers to an audience. The term "African American literature" refers to the ethnic backgrounds of the authors. When the two categories are combined into one—African American children's literature—the parameters are not clear at all. This confusion with defining this literature is important because of the deliberate uses to which it is put.

Young people, unlike adults, do not always have choice in the selection of their reading materials. Teachers or parents might choose a book with the specific intention that it be used to teach about a particular Black historical figure or era, or to represent values that they want to emphasize or instill in children. They place a certain degree of blind trust in an author whom they assume shares, to some extent, a common history or culture. They will be disappointed, to say the least, after choosing a young adult novel, perhaps in reaction to a cover illustration of Black characters, only to find that that the cover is misleading.

Kristin Hunter's *The Soul Brothers and Sister Lou* (1969) is just one example of how the publishing industry is just that—a business—with marketing strategies and concerns about profit margins and the like. The main character is light-skinned, a fact that she mentions and that makes a difference in her story. On the cover, she is depicted as a dark-skinned girl. My guess is that this was a marketing department decision with the underlying reasoning that during the "black is beautiful" movement, a book with a dark-skinned girl on the cover would sell well. My negative reaction is to what appears to be the business side of this book's history. The story itself is wonderful. A much more problematic example is the case in which parents or teachers choose a book simply because they see Black faces on the front, only for their children to be bombarded with gross insults upon reading.

Consider, for instance, Louise Fitzhugh's *Nobody's Family is Going to Change* (1974), later transformed into the Broadway hit "The Tap Dance Kid." When Emma, one of the protagonists, labels her brother "the nigger Nijinsky" because of his love for dancing, the mother's retort is a weak (in context) "Emma, that's the worst thing I ever heard in my life. Now you apologize right this minute!" The passage becomes more and more problematic, with Willie declaring that "nigger" is "better than faggot" and Emma following her mother's order to apologize, continuing with "Oh, little brother, friend of the white man, I meant you no harm. I would not hurt a nap on your nappy head." I doubt that an African American author would write such a scene.

Equally problematic are books such as Hadley Irwin's *I Be Somebody* (1984) which not only misuses Black English Vernacular grammatical constructions, but also implies throughout the book that the protagonist is not "somebody" inherently, but must become "somebody." Ann Cameron's *The Stories Julian Tells* (1981) and its several sequels is based upon stories told to the author by a young Black family friend of hers. However, in conversation with me, the author admitted that to avoid the possibilities of faulty retellings or misrepresentation, she does not include in these stories any culturally specific speech or details. In my estimation, this approach certainly insures the creation of oftentimes sterile, boring stories. Misrepresentation and objectification of Black characters reaches an extreme in William Armstrong's *Sounder* (1969) in which

Sounder, a dog, is the only character in the story who possesses a proper name. The Black family is referred to only as "the mother," "the father," "the boy," and so forth, rendering them worse than stereotypes.

One of the most well-known examples of controversy over white authorship is the statement made by critic Bob Dixon (1977, p. 123) about Ezra Jack Keats's *The Snowy Day* (1962):

> [The characters] are black enough, but it's only skin deep. Nothing would be affected in Keats' stories if the characters were white. The whole social, political, and cultural significance of being black is left out. In fact, as Ray Anthony Shepard remarked in the United States publication, *Interracial Books for Children*, "*Snowy Day* said that Black kids were human by presenting them as colored white kids."

I argue, in fact, that Keats's work does, indeed, speak to many African American children if only through a pictorial and sometimes textual couching in an urban context, or through the illustration of children with brown skin. (Of course, urban does not equal African American. Neither does brown skin. Both equations have a negative history). It is because of the existence of (unlike Keats's work) the more blatantly or insidiously negative treatments of Black people that I contend that there must be that which is consciously "African American" alongside that which is "culturally neutral"—every piece of African American literature does not have to be *about* being Black. In any case, the real usefulness of Dixon's standpoint is that it isolates some relevant issues.

If for "progressive" white authors and illustrators the priority is merely to disseminate non-stereotypical, "universal" images of African American people, then the emphasis for many African

American authors is different. Their priority is not only to create positive images but to create identifiably, authentic African American images which acknowledge and celebrate differences as well as similarities in black communities. A society's art is, ultimately, an expression of its self image, its values, its ways of thinking, behaving, viewing itself. Art is a means of preserving and passing on this image and legacy, the implications of which can not always be understood fully by white authors or illustrators.

All of the foregoing discussion is not just philosophical, but quite real in broader context. One huge problem is that, historically, white authors have been accepted not only as the creators of literature about or aimed at Black youth but, moreover, have been encouraged to fill this role. Twenty-five years ago, it was deplorable that art directors would tell acclaimed illustrator Tom Feelings that he was limiting himself by drawing only African American subjects. It is equally deplorable that one semester my students asked whether or not he illustrates white people too. What are the implications of their question? Even more to the point is the case of writer Eloise Greenfield who has it written into her contracts that her books must be illustrated by African American illustrators. We can safely infer, I think, that this means good Black illustrators.

Certainly, artists of all kinds have the right to work with whatever subject matter they choose. And just as there are African American artists who do not depict Black people successfully, there are white artists who do. However, it raises questions when certain writers or illustrators take it as their whole careers to re-tell stories other than "their own" stories. It is even more problematic when arrogant, ethnocentric editors presume, when choosing from equally talented white and black or other ethnic writers and illustrators, that the white artist is better equipped to tell an African American story or a Native American story; what they are presuming, essentially, is that the European American point of view is the most valuable, or maybe just the least threatening. African American and other ethnic artists find themselves in a catch 22. Often, the only way out of this predicament is through publishing with independent Black publishing companies, which have a whole host of problems with things such as distribution, but which are becoming more and more successful. I want to mention some of these houses.

There are several mainstream publishing houses which are actively looking for writers and illustrators (a la sixties and seventies style contests sponsored by the Interracial Council on Children's Books) instead of claiming that they don't exist. But it shouldn't always take political pressure such as that generated during the "black is beautiful" or multicultural movement to instigate such action. Publishers shouldn't rest easy with the racist assumption that a few successful people are exceptions— that they (editors) have found all of the capable Black writers and illustrators.

In this context, I should mention the Coretta Scott King Award, administered by the American Library Association's Social Responsibility Roundtable. On the list of Coretta Scott King Award winners, the same names appear again and again. Certainly many of these winners are outstanding, important writers and illustrators. But it will be nice when the list becomes more inclusive, indicating an increase of working African American creators of children's books. Another issue is the very idea of awards and the functions they serve. How do we read the fact that there is a special award for African Americans? What kinds of dynamics does its existence set up? I won't offer a response right now, but I offer the issue for thought. In any case, it is important that there **are** African American writers and illustrators depicting and interpreting the full range of African American experience. At the same time that we continue to celebrate and buy the classics, editors and art directors must be willing to take chances on more new artists. But they must not simply replace the old guard with a small new guard. They must constantly search out and develop talent while, yes, keeping ethnicity in mind. We do not live in a fairytale, color-blind world.

When looking closely at the facial illustrations by Carole Byard in Eloise Greenfield's *Grandmama's Joy* (1980), we can see power in the way that the face is almost luminous in its darkness, in its blackness. When the Kenneth and Mamie Clark doll experiments first conducted in the forties were repeated recently, the same results were found—African American children expressed a preference for white dolls; they somehow and for some reasons considered white dolls superior to the non-white. Or at least they thought that this was the preferred response. Because of the way in which the word "black" is used and conceptualized in our language and culture, acclaimed children's writer Lucille Clifton finds it necessary to write in *Some of the Days of Everett Anderson* (1970) a verse such as this one in which her character Everett Anderson thinks:

> Afraid of the dark
> is afraid of Mom
> and Daddy
> and Papa
> and Cousin Tom.
> "I'd be as silly,
> as I could be,
> afraid of the dark
> is afraid of me!"
> says ebony Everett Anderson.

Because in *The Story of Little Black Sambo* Helen Bannerman
used the term "black" indiscriminately, pointlessly, and thus
destructively, Clifton (1970) is forced to write a poem asking the
rhetorical but ultimately meaningful question:

Who's black
and runs
and loves to hop?
Everett Anderson does.

Who's black
and was lost
in the candy shop?
Everett Anderson was.

Who's black
and noticed the
peppermint flowers?
Everett Anderson did.

Who's black
and was lost for
hours and hours?
Everett Anderson
       Hid!

Because of the realities of the society in which we live, Clifton
finds it necessary to reconceptualize the notion of blackness,
which she does both effectively and eloquently, again, through
the life of Everett Anderson (1970):

Daddy's back
is broad and black
and Everett Anderson loves to ride it.

Daddy's side
is black and wide
and Everett Anderson sits beside it.

Daddy's cheek
is black and sleek
and Everett Anderson kisses it.

Daddy's space
is a black empty place
and Everett Anderson misses it.

Finally, I want to share with you Everett Anderson's thoughts
when it is time to return to school in September of *Everett
Anderson's Year* (1974, n.p.):

I already know where Africa is.
And I already know how to count to ten.
I went to school every day last year.
Why do I have to go again?

My response to this is that it is clear that for Everett,
knowledge of Africa is just as fundamental as the skill of
counting. His sense of self and identity is secure, and this is
evident to any reader. This fact, for the young African American
reader, functions as a stabilizing and assuring force. For the
non-black reader, on the other hand, it should merely accentuate
the characterization, thus proving in no way threatening to a
reader's own sense of identity. What we call African American
children's literature may offer something special to young people
of African descent. But it is, ultimately, for any and all readers.
white children are harmed and deprived, too, when they get a
limited view of this richly diverse society and world of which we
are a part.

What happens in the world of the children's literature
publishing industry, in concert with formal and informal
educational institutions, has far-reaching political implications.
Chosen for them, the literature to which children are exposed in
the school system is often their first contact with literature. If
this is a negative experience, if they never read stories or see
illustrations that reflect their lives, they may not, in the present
or the future, develop any kind of appreciation for this form of
art, which has so much to offer. More dangerously, they may
never acquire the skills of literacy. Just as significantly, children
are not only educated, but miseducated through formal
educational channels. Just to be very clear—I acknowledge that
one function of literature is to introduce readers to worlds they
could experience in no other way. But a primary function of
literature is to offer us all representations and interpretations of
ourselves, as cultures and as individuals. Children's literature
can be a powerful tool of transmission not just of harmless,
innocent yarns, but of interpretations of histories and ideologies.
These issues are increasingly important as the demographics of
this country change, reflecting an increase of young students and
readers who are members of various ethnic groups. There is no
room for distortions of the real meaning of multiculturalism.
There is room, and there is an audience for a multiplicity of
voices.

We must advocate, in every way possible, the creation,
visibility, and accessibility of African American children's and
young adult literature. It is easy in our complex, problem-ridden
society of the 1990s to be pessimistic, concluding that there is no
such period as "childhood" for countless young people. What
we must remember, however, is that writers and illustrators are,
quite powerfully, reflecting these realities in their work.

Black adults as well as non-Black adults, in their many roles, must insist that this literature be reflected and utilized in school curricula and represented on book store shelves (ask your local bookseller to stock them!) These books should be on our shelves at home, as well as at school. Only then can they fulfill their potential.

It is a mistake to underestimate the power of books. Literature and art has been known to change or redirect an individual's life or a society's consciousness. The very existence of this body of work should be celebrated. For at its best, it consistently and profoundly shares some word or idea, some visual or narrative interpretation which holds enduring value for a most special audience, those whom DuBois called "the children of the sun."

I'd like to close by sharing with you Tom Feelings' and Eloise Greenfield's *Daydreamers* (1981). Part of Mr. Feelings' intention in collecting these drawings into one volume was to force us all simply to look, really look, at the faces of our young people. May we all be inspired by these words and images, and then DO something with this inspiration:

Daydreamers

holding their bodies still
for a time
letting the world turn around them

while their dreams hopscotch,
doubledutch
dance,

thoughts rollerskate,
crisscross,
bump into hopes and wishes.

Dreamers
thinking up new ways, looking toward new days,

planning new tries,
asking new whys.
Before long,
hands will start to move again,

eyes turn outward,
bodies shift for action,
but for this moment they are still,

they are
the daydreamers,
letting the world dizzy itself
without them.

Scenes passing through their minds
make no sound
glide from hiding places
promenade and return
silently

the children watch their memories
with spirit-eyes
seeing more than they saw before
feeling more
or maybe less
than they felt the time before

reaching with spirit-hands
to touch the dreams
drawn from their yesterdays.

They will not be the same
after this growing time,
this dreaming.
In their stillness they have moved
forward

toward womanhood
toward manhood.

This dreaming has made them new.

References

Clifton, L. (1974). *Everett Anderson's year.* Illustrated by Ann
    Grifalconi. NY: Holt, Rinehart and Winston.
_____. (1970). *Some of the days of Everett Anderson.*
    Illustrated by Evaline Ness. NY: Holt, Rinehart and
    Winston.
Dixon, B. (1977). *Catching them young: Sex, race and class in
    children's fiction.* London: Pluto.
Du Bois, W. E. B. (February 1921). "The grown-ups' corner."
    The Brownies' Book, 2, p. 63.
_____. (October 1919). "The true brownies." *The Crisis,* 6, pp.
    285-286.
Fauset, J. R. (January 1920). "Dedication." *The Brownies'
    Book*, 1, p. 32.
Feelings, T., and E. Greenfield. (1981). *Daydreamers.* NY:
    Dial.
Johnson, D. (1990). *Telling tales: The promise and pedagogy of
    African American literature for youth.* NY: Greenwood.

Ringgold, F. (1991). *Tar beach*. NY: Crown.
Sinnette, E. (1965). "The brownies' book: A pioneer
   publication for children." *Freedomways*, 5, pp. 133-142.

WHO'S GOING TO INTERPRET PERFORMANCE STANDARDS? A CASE FOR TEACHER JUDGMENT

Mary A. Barr

"A sentence uttered makes a world appear/Where all things happen as it says they do." So said W. H. Auden (1962), attesting to the power of the word, whether written or spoken. Those of us who applaud the current move toward the use of narrative statements of performance standards by which to assess and communicate the extent of student learning happily greet such power in persuading a concerned public that schools merit their trust. Even the most optimistic among us must consider, however, the implicit danger of which Auden warns: Words create their own realities, reliant for their meanings on speakers and listeners, readers and writers who share the experience represented in them. No less abstract than numbers, which belie their seeming objectivity, statements of expectations about student achievement are—let's face it—subject to interpretation, to mean, in paraphrase of the Red Queen, whatever individual users of language intend them to mean.

In 1994, when the California Learning Assessment System (CLAS) produced a set of performance standards and open ended tests for assessing their achievement, teachers and other educators who had worked on their formulation were dismayed by the outcry not only from many of their uninvolved colleagues, who saw the standards as alien and destructive of present instructional practices, but also from politicians, parents and community members who charged the California Department of

Education with intrusion into essentially private matters. Thus, an assessment of reading, writing, and mathematics designed to elicit thoughtful, student-constructed responses to text and actual experience elicited, instead, loud resistance and quick consignment to the innovation dust heap.

In hindsight, the cause of the demise of CLAS is clear and instructive. Although hundreds, perhaps thousands, of educators participated in and spoke for the testing reform effort, the reality of its implementation brought questions most thought they had answered and concerns most believed had been addressed. But words "make worlds appear," and local interpretations of the words in the standards and on the tests created worlds in which many people saw the requests for open response to text, for instance, as attempts by a faceless governmental bureaucracy to control the vulnerable minds of children. In their experience, after all, unbiased tests require single answers to multiple choice questions. The idea that given texts might provoke multiple interpretations, all of which could meet the truth test, disturbs their picture of testing—and of schooling.

CLAS-like alternatives to multiple-choice testing seem stymied in California for now, but the case against filling in the bubbles remains indisputable. Their use as the major arbiter in determining the levels of student achievement narrows the curriculum to what can be easily and cheaply measured. What's more, the need for secrecy of on-demand test items prevents the assessment of student performance over an extended time in realistic settings conducive to the creation of thoughtful responses and/or products. That these tests of low level skills and content, often mistakenly referred to as "the basics," have driven what happens in schools for more than two decades now is alarming, though not surprising. Lacking other means to account for program design and funding expenditures, districts have had to rely on the results of commercially-prepared, single response, on-demand tests for reporting to their publics about student achievement. The promise that schools will be able to loosen the grip of standardized testing on teaching and learning is well worth a careful, reasoned move toward the use of performance standards.

But standards require words, I remind you, and words project an inevitably subjective quality, full of the bias and undependability which promoted the development of the standardized testing industry in the first place. In this postmodern world, where subjectivity is generally acknowledged as part and parcel of any human endeavor, an assessment system must, more than ever before, provide assurance that equitable judgments of student achievement can be made. Judgments about student work must be made against commonly-agreed upon criteria and must leave no doubt as to their fairness and accuracy. Held to a higher standard than traditional test scores, which sought only to rank students along a bell curve, performance-based assessment must be, at one and the same time, less intrusive in classroom learning and more encouraging of academic rigor.

In this paper, I hope to spell out how two key elements of the California Learning Record (CLR) system of assessment[1] can help educators overcome the interpretation hazards posed by the use of performance standards in the assessment of students, K-12. The elements—a set of coherent principles and a system of validation for classroom assessments—work together to ensure that statements of performance standards do not become mere hurdles for students, constraints for teachers, and empty promises to parents and the general public.

Overview of the CLR Assessment System

The CLR system of assessment acknowledges that student use of language and literacy is fundamental to academic progress across the curriculum. Therefore, classroom teachers using the CLR, in concert with parents and students themselves, collect and document abundant evidence of what students, K-12, show they are learning as they talk, listen, read, and write in natural settings, as opposed to test-taking environments. Teachers collect and organize information about students' learning from multiple sources, using five-point scales of literacy performance for grade spans K-3, 4-8, and 9-12. Students and—with grade school age children, especially—their parents contribute to the accumulating data, which is gathered in a computerized or printed format. The data include documented observations, analyses of work samples from student discussions, presentations, reading responses and writing, both imaginative and informational, both text- and experience-related.

With the help of an experienced CLR teacher leader as school coach, teachers summarize the documented evidence collected throughout the year; they make judgments about student achievement using the CLR performance scales. Since their judgments grow out of their observations of students engaged in classroom activities and projects throughout the year, they can modify their instruction, e.g., changing its pace, altering topics, supplying information. At the end of the year, achievement summaries and scale placements inform students and their parents of the extent of student progress. In addition, the scale scores can be aggregated not only to monitor student achievement across grade levels but to effect the changes necessary to schoolwide program improvement.

The systematic flow from classroom learning use to school accountability purposes incorporates the perspectives of parent, student and teacher, creating a multi-faceted picture of achievement. The standardized format; a three year phase-in plan for professional development; an on-site coach, experienced in the use of the CLR; exemplars of student records; and a teacher handbook with rationale and classroom examples of student work and teacher commentary—all these facets of the system contribute to a locally-owned but fully informed picture of student literacy achievement which can be interpreted across school, district, and state levels. The picture is both qualitative and quantitative, with placement on performance scales by the classroom teacher validated in readings in the school and across schools.

Principles of CLR Assessment

The set of principles which guides the CLR system of assessment of student performance begins with the notion that *students must be assessed in favorable contexts,* that is, in situations in which they can demonstrate their capabilities. The rationale for this principle has to do with fairness and the validity of the assessment. Students have a right to be able to show what they know and can do on tasks which reflect not only school and community priorities but also their own strengths and interests. Psychometric approaches to assessment deal with fairness by requiring standardized administration and equivalent tasks for all, but, as Moss points out, there is still a question of "differential familiarity" which handicaps some students (1994, p. 9).

With the CLR, teachers seek evidence of learning as students work on given or self-selected tasks in the familiar classroom setting where the context can support students as they add new knowledge to their present understandings. As Barnes (1987) makes clear, "Apart from rote memorizing, all learning takes place through changes in the learner's existing model of the world." If assessment is to support student learning, it follows that it must document those changes in the learner's model of the world as well as the teacher's. "What is required," he says, "is the opportunity for pupils to try out their new understandings, to talk, make diagrams, calculate, so that the new modifies the old while at the same time the old plays its essential part in understanding the new" (p. 28).

Lynda Peddy, a reading specialist who works with teachers in several schools near Sacramento, provides an example of how the opportunity Barnes speaks of can also provide information about student progress. Using the CLR Data Collection form, Lynda noted that Jennifer, a first grader, "worked throughout writer's workshop, writing and drawing for about 20 minutes. She used invented spelling without over concern for perfection." She also saw that "Jennifer used both beginning and ending sounds of words to help her spell unfamiliar words when writing." From this single observation, Lynda could tell that Jennifer had not only developed the confidence and independence necessary to concentrate on a single task but that she knew enough about the sounds of print symbols to use them in constructing her own text. A week later, working on another topic, Jennifer demonstrated her growing sense that her writing must be conventional enough that others could read what she wrote. She reread her text and inserted an omitted "n" in the word *friend*, thereby revising her original text. Lynda documented these demonstrations of developing literacy to describe Jennifer's particular progress in becoming a reader and writer and, at the same time, to help her decide how she might provide Jennifer with further opportunity to learn. At the end of the year, she, with the classroom teacher, would look for patterns of growth across many such observations to determine and record Jennifer's literacy achievement in comparison with other first graders. She will then be able to help her second grade teacher build on Jennifer's accomplishments.

A second CLR principle is that *students be assessed across a range of social and learning situations* in order that (1) teachers can support emerging skills and subject matter knowledge and (2) they can ensure that students gain experience with the demands placed on literacy, both in form and substance, in different settings. For example, the kinds of language needed in a peer group discussion about the impact of an historical event on modern culture contrasts with the language required to use the same event as evidence for an opinion in a persuasive essay for adult readers. To note student capabilities in different social/learning contexts, CLR teacher observations and student reflections document language and literacy learning in individual, paired, and group settings; with adults and peers; live or recorded; formal, informal; in subject areas across the curriculum.

In her San Diego classroom, Carol Sandstrom, for instance, documented evidence of Jason's literacy development as the third grader worked on eight reading and writing tasks during the year in a variety of settings:

Reading Observation Notes

Sept.	small group	Met with group to practice 3-part presentations of fable. J. interacted as they negotiated the parts.
Feb.	small group	Leader of group to practice reading *Rumpelstiltskin* to present to the class.

Group drew cards indicating parts. J. read his part fluently & helped others with words.

Feb. paired   Read "The Princess and the Critter" to partner as an introduction to storytelling. Read with ease and confidence.

Apr. large   Poetry reading of "Sunshine Cake" in
group   unison. Read clearly with expression.

Apr. individually   Selected Nature's Watch; knows how to use table of contents

Writing Observation Notes

Sept. individually   Entries in learning log indicate interests in swimming, trips to the beach—"the type of weather that is like me is summer." Enjoys science—snakes & lizards; included a diagram of a piranha showing sharp teeth & description below. Writes short entries of one or two sentences with illustrations.

Dec. paired   Used his planning sheet to outline an
peer &   original fable—met with response partner,
adult   then teacher for final editing. Inserted a sentence that enhanced his story.

Apr. individually   Has shown a recent interest in writing a "chapter" story in his journal—keeps asking "When can I write? When are we having journal writing?" Ability to sustain writing for longer periods is evident.

These observations, along with a range of reading and writing samples from his portfolio of work, helped Carol conclude that Jason had become a fluent reader (a "4" on a five point scale) at the end of third grade. Using the performance criteria for Grades K-3 (see Appendix) as general descriptors of developmental stages in learning to read, she summarized the specific evidence of the breadth of his reading and writing to justify her judgment of his reading achievement:

> He selects books on nature and wildlife as well as poetry and narrative. He is an experienced reader and shows interest and ability to locate books in the library. He selected the *Three Little Pigs* by Wm. Hooks, recognizing the similarities and differences from the traditional book that was given him at a younger age. He appreciated this version from the Appalachian story tellers and could relate the characters' actions with his life. When reading a page from *Different Dragons* by Jean Little [district-recommended for fourth grade], he was very expressive, and on two occasions of running records, he did not miss a word.

A third principle, *that assessment must attend to both process and product,* complements large scale, externally designed assessment which relies on post hoc examination of student work without first-hand knowledge of the conditions under which it was done. As Syverson notes (Syverson, 1994), knowing the context or ecology of the composing situation is critical in understanding the extent to which the composition succeeds. Not only did Lynda, in her observations noted earlier, describe what product Jennifer was creating but also how persistently she attended to the task she had set for herself. Further, she could evaluate accurately what the series of illustrated stories Jennifer produced revealed about her learning because she knew just what Jennifer intended to express.

Similarly, Jason's teacher knew that he comprehended grade level texts because she heard him read expressively and fluently and she checked his understanding with a running record. Jason also demonstrated he could orally interpret text when he read to others because he could supply his listeners with the intonations they needed for comprehension.

Fourth in the list of CLR system principles is that assessment must acknowledge the integral role of language in learning. The processes of speaking and listening, reading and writing both demonstrate and promote learning. The brief samples from Jason's and Jennifer's records exemplify how the use of language, written and spoken, reveal to their teachers just what they are coming to know and learning to do. That language use both fosters and reveals learning is an intuitively congruent notion buttressed in the seminal works of such thinkers as Vygotsky (1978), Britton (1992), and Bruner (1990). The idea flies in the face of much current pedagogical practice, however. Darling-Hammond (1985), for instance, reports that instruction is increasingly strait-jacketed by tests and packaged instructional programs which standardize teaching practices and, I must add, prevent students from using their language to make sense of new knowledge:

> [Teachers] spend less time on untested subjects, such as science and social studies; they use less writing in their classrooms in order to gear assignments to the format of standardized tests; they resort to lectures rather than classroom discussions in order to cover the prescribed behavioral objectives without getting "off the track;" they are precluded from using teaching materials that are not on prescribed textbook lists, even when they think these materials are essential to meet the needs of some of their students; and they feel constrained from following up on

expressed student interests that lie outside the bounds of mandated curricula (p. 209).

And Goodman (1995) also describes the effects of this standardization of tests and programs on teachers, who are, for many children, important models in learning the language of cognition. He charges:

> Instead of being intellectually engaged with curriculum content and student learning, teachers using these instructional programs [standardized materials] merely administer the day's activities efficiently to ensure that pupils "get through" the program on time. Such activities include scheduling time for each subject and ability group, planning seat work to keep children busy, selecting special worksheets to address individual students' deficiencies, assisting students who have difficulty with a given task, disciplining pupils to keep them on task, and maintaining pupils' records. Many of these instructional programs are so finely tuned that teachers no longer actually need to "teach"—that is, teachers do not have to conceptualize content or navigate children's learning (p. 11).

In addition to the important function that teachers serve as models of the language *of* learning, they also have the authority to encourage or discourage the use of language *in* learning. When they do all the directing and assigning in the classroom, they are not providing opportunities for students to build on what they already know. Without opportunity to use language to explore new knowledge, students cannot demonstrate what they are learning, so assessment, in these classrooms, cannot reflect what many, perhaps most, students know and can do. What's more, teachers, without knowing what students know, cannot provide the opportunities students need to comprehend academic language in the context of its use.

A newsletter from the Association for Supervision and Curriculum Development (Willis, 1995) featured an article recently about the large gap between what's needed and what's customary in the teaching of science. A description of an exemplary eighth grade earth science classroom, for instance, illustrated how students are called upon to use their own language (reading, writing, speaking and listening) as a part of the recommended "hands-on" activities:

> [Students in this example are participating in an international ozone monitoring project.] Using filter-paper badges, students collect smog data locally and then share their findings via the Internet with students at 80 other schools around the world...students also graph and analyze the data. In the process, they learn vocabulary such as "nitrous oxide" and "parts per billion" without having to resort to rote memorization. Students also submit their data to the Air Quality Board, the governor, and the National Student Research Center. Because they care about air quality, and because they are collecting real data to be shared with others, students take their work seriously (p. 1).

The tasks may seem exotic to those not equipped, either intellectually or financially, for the blessings of the "information highway" depicted in this short account. The "international" nature of the project, the use of the Internet, and the submission of results to national and state audiences may seem, to some, undoable in "regular" classrooms, but the picture can still serve to exemplify purposeful, engaging activity the bare bones of which it is possible to replicate in every school. Complex kinds of language and cognition thrive and develop when they serve the purposes of students who are analyzing and sharing findings, using content vocabulary, and submitting data to significant audiences. Students in these settings demonstrate their language capabilities as they

- actively seek meaning in the data being gathered, simultaneously orchestrating prior and new knowledge as they share their findings,
- bring their skills and strategies to bear on comprehending and composing text for real purposes, and
- dare to err, knowing that errors provide information which can be discussed, analyzed and used.

That students are also gaining subject matter skills and knowledge in such classrooms as this one recommended for science teaching and learning is clear to me and, I believe, to most. The problem of implementing such rich classroom experience, however, is that it is not endorsed by the conventional testing programs. Parents, teachers, and students, therefore, often see their efforts as "extra," outside the real agenda for schooling. If, on the other hand, practices like those illustrated were legitimated by an assessment system like the CLR, students and their teachers would, as educational reformers urge, engage in solving authentic problems requiring high levels of literacy.

The fifth and final CLR principle is that *performance criteria must be shared among stake-holders* if assessment is to truly improve teaching and learning for all students. Secrecy surrounding test making and test taking, however, has always been the norm. Only recently, with the advent of performance assessment, have questions about test content surfaced in public debate. California's education code, for example, has for years insisted on "secure" test items and the public has not questioned their substance. Although charges of cheating on multiple choice tests at the military academies and in high schools have frequently made headlines, the attitude in the reports is that it is the students, not the tests, which must be investigated.

As Badger (1995) explains, this lack of scrutiny has perpetuated the status quo:

> The use of normative scores, as well as the exclusive use of multiple-choice questions, has effectively barred the public from the educational discourse. By cloaking results in the language of psychometrics, professional educators, including state governments, have controlled the interpretation of testing.... The rationale for...discrepancies in performance has been laid at the feet of the students themselves, and has been justified by test results (p. 342).

The use of performance standards promises to counteract the damaging effects of traditional testing and, as Badger puts it, "to shift the focus of equity from individuals who are seen as educationally deficient, to school practices which reinforce that deficiency" (p. 342). When student achievement is measured against performance standards, the tests themselves, it seems, are indeed called into question. In the case of CLAS, for example, secrecy about test items and their scoring created such suspicion among concerned citizens as to what students were being asked to learn in school that rumors about mind control conspiracies overwhelmed reason. While I prefer this public response over that which condemns the students, it is nevertheless misdirected and stems, I contend, from the fact that the standards have not been interpreted locally—by the teachers, parents, and students who must judge and be judged by them.

The CLR, like all performance-based assessments, uses narrative descriptors of levels of achievement at different grade levels. It is, however, a completely open record in which student performance is documented throughout the year by all who have a stake in the success or failure of the student. Parents contribute what they know about student learning and literacy at home as well as what they would like to see the student be able to do; students describe themselves as learners and provide evidence in their portfolios and journals about current demonstrations of what is being learned; teachers collect these data and add their own observations and analyses of student work compiled in the student record.

It should be pointed out here that the CLR collects evidence only of what students have demonstrated they know and can do. Since judgments of performance are based on what has actually been demonstrated and recorded in the record, there are no speculations about any deficits the student may have. The K-3 reading scale, included as an appendix to this paper, illustrates how this affirmative action works. The "beginning reader" is defined as one who:

> Uses a few successful strategies for tackling print independently. Relies on having another person to read the text aloud. May still be unaware that text carries meaning.

Raul's teacher assessed him two-thirds of the way through the kindergarten year as being at this stage of becoming a reader. She had written in January that his "pictures are gradually starting to correspond to dictation," using a picture of Goldilocks as evidence. She found him "starting to use environmental print" as denoted by his copying the word *chick* from a label in the room. A few days later he copied "futterfly" and drew a butterfly to go with it, thereby indicating he is beginning to recognize that "text carries meaning." Around the same time, Raul showed his teacher the book *Eensy Weensy Spider* saying, "Look, teacher, I can read!" That he sang the song without looking at or pointing to the words signaled to her that he was not yet connecting specific print symbols and their sounds. He did, however, she noted, recognize the book title. By April, the teacher found that Raul could read to her what he had written under one of his drawings. He also listened without distraction to a book she had read to the whole class previously, even knew the word "cocoon" in the story and remembered the sequence of events.

All of these signs of emerging literacy or "successful strategies for tackling print independently" denote progress toward independent reading and, at the same time, suggest steps the teacher and parent can take to further support his development. The written record of what Raul demonstrates he can do serves as a series of clues to what he is learning to do and the developmentally sound performance scale indicates how he can be helped to learn more.

Contrast this kind of assessment with one made of Robert's achievement. Representative of the kind of assessment which focuses on deficits rather than on demonstrated performance, the record illustrates just how flawed and unhelpful a genre it is. Robert, a second grader, was examined by a school psychologist in what he described as a "structured testing setting" to determine whether or not Robert should be put in special classes for the "learning disabled." On-demand test results for reading showed Robert "confuses similar words, disregards punctuation, guesses words, hesitates, inserts extra words, loses [his] place, mispronounces words, omits words, [uses] poor phrasing, reverses words, substitutes words, fails to syllabicate words, and [shows] poor use of word attack." No test content other than the test publisher's general statement of what the test purports to measure, e.g., basic reading skills, is given. Robert was placed in a special education class, in part, because of this uninterpreted reading test.

The five CLR principles discussed above underpin the CLR system of assessment. To review, they

- promote problem solving in and outside the classroom rather than anxiety-laden testing settings,
- provide experience across a range of social and learning situations rather than constraining performance to what can be easily and quickly measured,
- attend to both process and product rather than to post hoc examination of student work only,
- acknowledge the integral role of language in learning rather than isolating subject matter from its human expression, and
- provide for a sharing of the interpretations of performance criteria among teachers, parents and students rather than insisting on closeted interpretations by unidentified scorers.

These principles permit the development of a student assessment which is not only congruent with current views on learning but which also can link classroom assessment to demands for public accountability.

CLR System of Validation for Classroom Assessments

The CLR system of assessment presumes that the goal of schooling is to guide and support the development of independent learners who are confident, strategically skillful,

thoughtful, and habitually reflective about themselves as
learners. Teachers using the CLR, therefore, look for evidence
that students are becoming

- more confident and independent as learners,
- more able to use their prior knowledge and
  experience,
- more skilled and strategic in their school work,
- extending their knowledge and understandings, and
- more able to reflect on their own learning.

Lynda, whose experiences with Jennifer were cited earlier,
used these five dimensions to note, upon observation, that
Jennifer was using her home experiences with her mother and
sister to write and draw in school. Lynda documented Jennifer's
confidence and independence by noting that she took up her
work happily and persisted with it for an unusually long time
even though, as a first grader, she did not yet have all the skills
to communicate correctly. Her focus permitted her to complete
her work, to reflect on its intended effect and to revise it. Carol,
Jason's teacher, also provided specific evidence over the course
of the year that Jason was becoming independent (working
productively in a group and with a partner), was obviously
overcoming his shyness as he eagerly sought to extend his skills,
strategies, knowledge and understanding (asking to write more,
drafting and revising his work), and was progressing in his
ability to use his experience in and outside of school to enhance
his school work (defining his interests in his journal, reading
nature texts, collaborating with others).

These five dimensions of learning, then, provide a prism
through which teachers look for evidence of what students are
coming to know and are increasingly able to do. In so doing,
their teaching responds to and builds on student learning, the

desired outcome of formative assessment. The dimensions are also embedded in the CLR performance scales for reading and writing, making the scales useful in summative assessment. Carol was able to place Jason at the end of the year near the top of the K-3 reading scale, for instance, because her documentation of his behavior in class and her analysis of samples of his work throughout the year provided evidence that, among other Level 4 indicators, he chose to read silently and was beginning to draw inferences from books and stories.

Would other teachers, both in and outside the school, agree with Carol's placement of Jason on the reading scale of performance? Probably, yes, according to results from CLR site and regional "moderation" sessions held April-June at sites across California in 1994 and 1995. Teachers provided copies of student records from their classrooms, with selected work samples from student portfolios attached to each. They masked their own scale placements, and other teachers read their records in pairs, arriving at joint decisions about scale placements. Each pair discussed and sometimes modified individual interpretations of the performance scales for measuring reading achievement as they came to consensus about scale placement based on the evidence contained in the record at hand.

The process, called moderation, provides answers to the question, "How consistent are CLR teacher judgments of student progress?" Both years, the moderations, conducted regionally with results collected statewide, produced high rates of agreement. In 1995, for example, 135 judgments (79 percent) made by the originating classroom teachers were corroborated by two pairs of teachers. The remaining 35 records were ranked one point higher or lower and required another reading. Of the 198 submitted records, 20 placements could not be corroborated because regional readers determined that there was not enough evidence to assign a scale placement. A survey conducted after each of the five regional moderations pointed to the probable cause. For most of the 125 participating teachers, the year had brought not only their first moderation but also their first year of keeping individual student records meant to be understood by other educators beyond the classroom. The most common response teachers made to the moderation experience (66 of 84 respondents) was that the evidence to defend their judgments of student performance was known and available, but they had overlooked and omitted it. As one teacher put it, "I learned that it is important to justify observations with data. Children's perceptions of themselves as learners (quotes, comments), samples of their written work, and text samples is vital information to be included." With more experience in moderations, the consistency rate should rise, attesting to the reliability of teacher judgment when performance criteria and illustrative student evidence are locally interpreted.

With the CLR's proven capability to ensure the accuracy of classroom teachers' judgments about student achievement, the question of how to prevent teacher bias can be set aside in favor of another, more important question, "Does the CLR system of assessment improve teaching and learning?"

One of the criticisms of conventional assessments is that their use narrows the curriculum to what can be easily measured. To study the effects of the CLR and the moderations on classroom practice, teachers were asked to describe the changes they will make in their use of the CLR next year. A complete analysis of their responses is underway, but a preliminary look reveals that most plan to reorganize their classrooms to permit more student involvement in learning and assessment. One teacher, who described the moderation experience as "very intense and productive," spoke for many who learned just "what

I need to collect as evidence." Another said she needed "to look at class structure differently and modify teacher talk" because she "learned with these 3 students[2] what works with some and not others." Specifically, this teacher noted, "I need to make my room/lessons more student-centered.... This process has helped to redefine the teacher's role."

Another criticism of conventional assessments is that they require secrecy so they cannot provide useful, timely information. A school board member, having observed the moderation process, attested to the transparency of the records as to what's being taught and learned. "I'm told, 'They're not teaching reading anymore.' I can see by these records evidence of learning word attack skills, comprehension, etc. And I can use the scales when I visit classrooms." Appreciation of this open view of classroom learning was echoed by teachers, many of whom said things like this one: "It's great to be able to...look at other teachers' records, especially from teachers whom I don't usually work with, and learn about what they're doing and why they do it. It validates our roles not only as 'teachers' but as researchers, observers, and learners."

Among the positive comments, surprisingly few teachers expressed dismay at the profound nature of the changes in their practice the CLR requires. We hope to document, in studies underway, evidence of the kinds of school and regional support teachers need not only to meet the classroom challenges of more complex assessment like the CLR but to make their findings count for public accountability. It is my hunch, however, that what is needed is not some startling new technique, package or system but teachers, students, parents and the school community communicating about student work, what it means, what they are doing to improve it. The CLR system supports this notion by keeping the center of the action at the school level where standards can be interpreted in the light of local illustrations of what they mean and how they are being met.

Footnotes

1. The CLR is adapted with permission from the Primary Language Record (PLR) (copyright, 1988, ILEA/Centre for Language in Primary Education, Webber Row, London SE1 8QW). The PLR has been used in many London elementary schools since 1985 and is now being introduced in New York City. CLPE and the Center for Language in Learning work together to create the PLR/CLR assessment system.

2. The first year of using the CLR, teachers keep records on just three to five students in order to learn the system.

References

Auden, W. H. (1962). "Words." In O. Williams & E. Honig (Eds.), *The mentor book of major American poets*, (p. 520). NY: New American Library.

Badger, E. (1995). "The role of expectations and fairness in state wide assessment programs: Lessons from Massachusetts." In M. T. Nettles & A. L. Nettles (Eds.), *Equity and excellence in educational testing and assessment*. Boston, MA: Kluwer Academic Publishers, pp. 323-346.

Barnes, D., Britton, J., and Torbe, M. (1987). *Language, the learner and the school*. (3rd ed.). Harmondsworth, England: Penguin Books.

Britton, J. (1992). *Language and learning*. (2nd ed.). Portsmouth, NH: Boynton/Cook, Heinemann Publishers.

Bruner, J. (1990). *Acts of meaning*. Cambridge, MA: Harvard University Press.

Darling-Hammond, L. (1985). "Valuing teachers: The making of a profession." In *Teachers College Record*, 87, pp. 205-218.

Goodman, J. (1995). "Change without difference." In *Harvard Educational Review*, 65(1), pp. 1-29.

Moss, P. A. (1994). "Can there be validity without reliability?" *Educational Researcher*, 23(2), pp. 5-12.

Syverson, M. A. (1994). *The wealth of reality: An ecology of composition*. Unpublished dissertation, University of California at San Diego.

Vygotsky, L. S. (1978). *Mind in society: The development of higher psychological processes* (A. R. Luria, Trans.). Cambridge, MA: Harvard University Press.

Willis, S. (1995). *Reinventing science education: Reformers promote hands-on, inquiry-based learning* (Curriculum Update): Association for Supervision and Curriculum Development.

Appendix

❖ California Learning Record ❖

READING SCALE 1, GRADES K-3: BECOMING A READER

Dependence → Independence

Language 1 →

Language 2 →

1	2	3	4	5
Beginning reader	Not-yet-fluent reader	Moderately fluent reader	Fluent reader	Exceptionally fluent reader
Uses just a few successful strategies for tackling print independently. Relies on having another person to read the text aloud. May still be unaware that text carries meaning.	Tackling known and predictable text with growing confidence but still needing support with new and unfamiliar ones. Growing ability to predict meanings and developing strategies to check predictions against other cues such as the illustrations and the print itself.	Well-launched on reading but still needs to return to a familiar range of reader text. At the same time beginning to explore new kinds of texts independently. Beginning to read silently.	A capable reader who now approaches familiar texts with confidence but still needs support with unfamiliar materials. Beginning to draw inferences from books and stories. Reads independently. Chooses to read silently.	An avid and independent reader who is making choices from a wider range of material. Able to appreciate nuances and subtlety in text.

This scale has been adapted with permission for use in the California Learning Record assessment system with funding provided by the California Department of Education. Originally developed and copyrighted by the Centre for Language in Primary Education, Webber Row, London SE8QW, the scale appears in the Primary Language *Handbook for Teachers*, which is distributed in the U.S. by Heinemann Educational Books.

WHAT IS AFRICA TO ME?
A DISCURSIVE APPROACH TO
LITERACY AND THE
CONSTRUCTION OF TEXTS IN
THE BLACK ADOLESCENT
IMAGINATION

Garrett A. Duncan

What is Africa to me:
Copper sun or scarlet sea,
Jungle star or jungle track,
Strong bronzed men or regal black
Women from whose loins I sprang
When the birds of Eden sang...
What is Africa to me?
"Heritage," by Countee Cullen

Introduction

Literacy, the process of reading the word and the world, is a
vehicle by which subjugated people are able to transform the
conditions that bind them. In particular, literacy connects our
linguistic capacities as human beings to the acquisition of the
necessary skills that allow us to expand our possibilities for
living in and with a world of other people and things. "The word
literacy, then, suggests a state of being and a set of capabilities
through which the literate individual is able to utilize the *interior
world of the self to act upon and interact with the exterior*

structures of the world around him [or her] in order to make sense of self and other" (Courts, 1991, p. 4; original emphasis).

It is through language that our possibilities for literacy are realized. More than simply a system of thought and vocalization, language must be viewed as a terrain upon which revolutionary desires, aspirations, dreams, and hopes are given meaning through a merging of the discourses of critique and desire (Freire & Macedo, 1987). Indeed, the rules, or systems, which govern thought and language are shaped by the social, cultural, and historical contexts in which language is developed and acquired.

This article examines the discursive domain of language as it relates to literacy and the manner by which Black teenagers read the word as an extension of making sense of the world. The discursive dimension of language pertains to that deeply embedded plane of reasoning that makes it possible for us to critically perceive, interpret, and reconstruct reality. Discursive activities, then, refer to those semiotic devices and mediations—the process and product of historical conditioning—that we use to give meaning to the world (Bakhtin, 1981; Harre & Gillett, 1994; Wertsch, 1991). Thus, a discursive approach to literacy and the construction of texts in the Black adolescent imagination is at once epistemological, psychological, and, most critically, political.

A fundamental assumption to understanding a discursive approach to literacy is that Black teenagers are human beings. This premise is stated rather explicitly, not to question the humanity of a class of people, but to raise the issue of what it is to be human. With respect to the present discussion, the issue of humanity is raised in order to acknowledge our dialectically subjective and objective natures. Along these lines, to be human means to be able to reflect upon and transform a world that is, in turn, transforming us. In a society stratified by relations of power, this assumption is critical to understanding the tensions that result when individuals, and collectives, assert their agency in a social order defined by multiple constraints. It follows, then, that as we act to reconcile the contradictions that exist between public representations and our private realities, the process of literacy is directed at *transforming that which is transforming us.* As Jonathan Kozol (1986) points out, "literacy, so conceived, is civil disobedience in pedagogic clothes: a cognitive denunciation of dynastic power, an ethical affront to imperial injustice" (p. 92). Hence, the practice of literacy is essentially humanizing activity.

This conception of literacy is especially useful for articulating the nature of cultural dynamics in the United States, where domination along the lines of culture, class, age, and gender is a salient organizing principle. On several occasions, I have pointed out that resistance and self-determination, or *kujichagalia,* are salient values shaping the outlooks of an increasing number of Black adolescents coming of age in urban America, values steadily gaining prominence above those of compliance, conformity, and assimilation. What this means is that these individuals are reading the world in ways that are in direct conflict of dominant cultural realities. In a very complicated way, the discursive activities of these youths, or the ways in which they experience and construct life, imply a challenge to truth and knowledge, how we know, and what's worth knowing. These activities shall be examined below in terms of what and why Black teenagers call themselves what they do.

What is Africa to Me?
Political and Epistemological Considerations

In general, theories of teaching and learning must be linked to wider theories of ideology and the development of youth subjectivity. Particularly, the idea of literacy must be connected to the issues of cultural democracy and the reproduction of dominant systems of meaning-making in public schools. In terms of the first issue, Kozol (1986) addresses this when he asks,

> When nearly half of all adult Black citizens in the United States are coming out of public schools without the competence to understand the antidote instructions on a chemical container, instructions on a medicine bottle, or the books and journalistic pieces which might render them both potent and judicious in a voting booth, who can pretend that literacy is not political? (p. 92).

To understand the second issue, that is, the political nature of making meaning, especially as this dialectic plays out in schools, the notion of literacy must also be examined for how it "sets off and defines through the concept of *illiterate* what can be termed the 'experience of the other'" (Freire & Macedo, 1987, p. 12). Along this line, Henry Giroux goes on to state that "the concept illiterate in this sense often provides an ideological cover for powerful groups simply to silence the poor, minority groups, women, or people of color. Consequently, naming illiteracy as part of the definition of what it means to be literate represents an ideological construction informed by particular political interests" (p. 12).

The discursive concepts *objectivism, solipsism,* and *prolepsism* are used to link the process of meaning-making to the particular interests attached to what and why a group of Black teenagers I interviewed label themselves what they do. Briefly, as a way of knowing, objectivism tends to obviate the agency of men and women, in effect reducing us to flesh and blood. Consonant with this form of thinking is viewing the world as natural and unproblematic. Solipsism, as a way of making meaning, also underlies a diminished view of the agency of men and women. Solipsism, however, differs fundamentally from objectivism in that the former allows for the recognition of inequality and oppression and seeks to ameliorate conditions within a prescribed system. Prolepsism, finally, is a form of reasoning that suggests human agency. This structure of reasoning often underlies the ability of Black youth to deconstruct human interests attached to dominant systems of meaning-making and, moreover, to reconstruct themselves and, in effect, their realities.

In my view, the differences that exist between and contradictions in how we come know what we do—and what we recognize as true—has much to do with the type of discursive reasoning we employ to give meaning to the different circumstances we encounter. In suggesting discursive categories, though, I am not arguing for ideal types. Rather it is my view that how we engage the world has to do both with our personal discursive profiles (in a way similar to Howard Gardner's [1983] theory of multiple intelligences) and the circumstances of our lived experiences.

In terms of Black teenagers, a range of objectivist, solipsist, and prolepsist reasoning is indicated in what and why they call themselves what they do. For instance, to the question "how do you describe yourself culturally or ethnically or in terms of your race?," the following responses were given during different interviews:[1]

This is where I was born, I'm American—born in California. You know, I know my ancestors came from Africa and everybody else knows this. I guess you can say that I'm classified as an African American. *Gina, 18*

I'm Afro-American because my ancestors were originally from Africa. And I was not born in Africa; I was born in America. So I do have some African in me, so I consider myself an African-American. *Albert, 14*

I identify myself as American because I'm in America. I was born in America, so I'm like, I'm American. *Melvin, 15*

In these instances, the teenagers designate themselves what they do based on (1) where they were born or now live and/or (2) the land of their ancestors. To these individuals, being American or African American is a given and not an issue to be contested. As Gina goes on to note, "I have no problem with being an American Black child." Albert adds, in relation to what he calls himself, "we all bleed red blood—we're all the same inside; we're just coated, you know. That's the way I look at it."

Calling one's self American does not necessarily indicate that the person holds an unproblematic view of society. For instance, consider what Albert's brother Louis, 15, has to say along these lines:

Some people say they're Black, but some people will join gangs and say "white people are this" and "Black is this—gangs and drugs." But if you talking about an Afro-American student, they might think another way.

In his own words, Louis articulates the deeper social significations of calling himself what he does. In his view,

naming one's self in the United States may carry a range of
meanings, from those relating to character and respectability to
those concerning class and economics. Whereas Louis appears
to adopt codes of the dominant American society in naming
himself, other teenagers employ a form of reasoning similar to
his to explain why they do *not* call themselves American or
African American. For instance,

> I'm not to keen to African American. That's just what they
> are allowed to say on the news. You know what they really
> want to call us. *Temika, 17*

In a another interview, the following sentiments were expressed:

> I have a problem with people who come into this belief that
> they are African American or they're Americans or any such
> thing of the word. It's like they're insulted by being what
> they really are or even associating themselves with their own
> history. And that disturbs me by saying that they have no
> self-respect or respect for your own people. *Daniel, 16*

> They don't consider you an American, so how can you
> consider yourself an American? They don't even consider
> you a human being, so why would you adapt to what they
> are? *Veronica, 18*

In the above instances, the teenagers point not only to social
significations, but also to the political ones of calling themselves
what they do. Clearly, Daniel's reference to history cannot be
reduced to a time in the past, but must be viewed also in terms of
the social, political, and cultural dynamics of the past, present,
and future. David, 16, who participated in the interview with
Daniel and Veronica, attests to this reading of Daniel's view of
history. Along these lines, he notes: "Daniel said something

when we were having the discussion; it kind of opened my eyes. I remember what the saying was: If a cat has kittens in an oven, does that make them biscuits? You know, I said 'yeah, that's true.'"

Another issue, consistent with David's remarks, one of forced citizenship, was expressed on several occasions as a factor in the naming process of the Black teenagers with whom I spoke. For example, during separate interviews, the following views were shared with me:

I asked my mother what she considers herself and she's like "I consider myself Black. I'm not just an African; I'm not American—my citizenship, I didn't ask for it." When I look in the mirror I see this brown-skinned woman and in this society, in America, that's when they call you Black, when you're that, so that's what I am. *Monica, 17*

I would say Black because African American—because we are not Americans. We didn't choose to be Americans. We were here first, and they're naming our lands and giving us a name. We pick our own name. I couldn't say African, because they took me from my homeland, to this land. So I have to pick my own name. But it's associated with Africans. *Clifton, 17*

I was not asked to be brought over here, so I will never consider myself to be an American. And, ultimately, we are not black because of our skin tone. You can get the darkest brother: He is still not absolutely black; he might be light purple or something, but he is not black. White people are just trying to make us the opposite of them. *Kwesi, 17*

The social and political significations of being Black, African, or American are more often than not articulated in terms of their conceptual and concrete relationship to racism/white supremacy, as Kwesi alludes to immediately above. Regina, 17, Kwesi's partner, is explicit in this regard:

> I don't consider myself black, because that's black [pointing to an object]. And they say black is the color of evil and white is the color of purity and all that old stuff. That's the term the white man gave us.

Along a similar line, seventeen year old Irene notes that:

> When I was little, I wanted blond hair and blue eyes. And then I started learning about my culture and I was like "dang, I should be happy that I'm Black." Now I see white people go to Black museums; they try to get everything on Black people like they think that Black people are going to be extinct in the future. Now I'm something that everybody else wants to be. *Irene, 17*

The process of reclamation, as articulated by Irene, is a prominent aspect in the discourse of several Black teenagers. For instance, a number of those with whom I spoke saw themselves and their circumstances from the perspective of diasporan Africans as opposed to ethnic Americans. For instance, in one interview, according to the interlocutors:

> It depends on who I am with. If I'm with down-home brothers that are political, politically aware, conscious, then I prefer to use African. I just feel home with African. When you say African, it describes everything. To me, it describes my whole experience, it sums it up. *Louise, 18*

If I'm in a political setting, I use African, because it gets
your point across. Like in speeches or real political things,
that's when it comes into play with myself. A lot of people
don't understand: "Why you say—why you say African?"
A lot a times, people be so shallow that I rather just say
Black to you. *Veronica, 18*

I feel that I am African in every setting, in every situation,
and every thought that comes to my mind. I feel that I gave
up the Black when Jesse [Jackson] came up with the "all
claim African American" thing and said this is what we
should be. Because once he put the African American stem
on us as a people in this country, he automatically said that
all other names or all other identifications now and forever
will be void, and you must use this stem. I think I had to go
a step further and say hey, I'm tired of these bourgeoisie
niggers and I got to go to this African state. So, you know,
I'm an African on a political, on a spiritual, and on a mental
standpoint and in all aspects. *Daniel, 16*

The above views are consistent with those articulated by several
teenagers I spoke with. Indeed, there are those instances where
individuals refuse for one reason or another to designate
themselves solely as Africans:

I ain't no African, you know? I don't limit myself to one
continent, you know what I 'm saying, because the Black
man is universal. *Clayton, 16*

I feel that if I knew more about the continent of Africa. If I
was more educated and could sit there and—you see, I feel
that at this point I am not ready to call myself African until I
know more. I wouldn't like to be somewhere and someone
asks me if I'm African and start throwing questions at me—I

couldn't handle that and I'd look really stupid. So, I think that's in due time because I do plan on studying more. But I do like to know more because I know people who call themselves Africans and they are quite more educated than I am. *Temika*

The Politics of Meaning-Making

As powerfully stated by many of those above, a growing number of Black adolescents assail the use of "African-American" as a term to describe who they are personally and socially. Criticism is leveled on a variety of planes (spiritual, historical, and political) and clearly involves a discursive grid of reasoning that is at once epistemological and political. In most cases, the denunciation of one's American-ness is made with explicit reference to the relationship between the character of the United States and the symbols of white supremacy.

For example, those who repudiate the term African-American give explicit reasons that refer to the issues of domination, subjugation, imperialism, and coercion. To dismiss the resistance of Black youth who do not identify with America as simply reactionary or as the rantings of pseudo-radicals is to simply deny the humanity of these individuals or, in other words, their capacity to critically reflect upon reality, to decode contradictions between public representations and lived realities, and to employ the values of justice and reconciliation in coming to their conclusions.

Many teenagers, even those who identify themselves as American, stress the importance of Blackness and link this, historically and culturally, to stories told to them by significant, usually older, others and to their vicarious meditations of and/or actual visits to Africa. Moreover, several of those with whom I spoke express beliefs that society, that is, those who make up the dominant culture of this country, does not regard Black people as completely human or at least as civilized as white people. Hence, from their reading of the world, to be American to these individuals not only means to assimilate but means also to repress those attributes of Black identities that are the subject of denigration by the dominant society—namely language and bodies.

In a similar way, "Black," depending on how it is conceptualized, is also evaluated and analyzed for its historical and discursive associations with oppression. As indicated elsewhere, on several occasions participants refused to identify themselves as being Black, using as their reference points pitch-black colored objects. However, these individuals were not merely referring to coloration. These teenagers, asserting themselves as human beings endowed with vibrant subjectivities, explicated the nuances of racism/white supremacy in the social construction of reality. For individuals to reject the designation "Black" on the basis of its connotation as an inanimate object is a declaration of their humanity, that they are in fact endowed with powerful points of views. In addition, individuals also distance themselves from the color metaphors that denote evil and inferiority. In doing so, many Black youths who reject the label Black clearly do this to extricate themselves from things evil.

Even those who refuse to accept the name "African" more often than not connect their decision to a static image of Africa as a geographical landscape. Also, many teenagers consciously do not call themselves African based on their understanding of the dynamic nature of culture and history. Along these lines, they also indicate that to ascribe one's self the status of African bears the burden of understanding all that the name entails.

Hence, several teenagers declare a moratorium on naming themselves African until such time they are satisfied that they have met the knowledge requirements to qualify themselves to be called African.

In those few instances in which American is accepted as a label of identity, these students generally view American society as an open field of dreams or, in other words, an unproblematic and unified landscape of choices and opportunities. From an epistemological standpoint, these students operate within the sphere of cognitive interests which give rise to the social mandate of *individualism* and the political requirement of *pluralism*. Although, for the most part, these students are considered successful in school and society and may seem to have a vested interest in the system as it is, this rationale does not generalize to all students. There are other teenagers who accept the label American and who are not "successful" in the system as it is. Further, even some of those who identify themselves as African or Black also hold views that mirror their African-American and American peers.

Conclusion: Concerning Pedagogy

The views expressed by an increasing number of Black teenagers suggest that the general ideas that undergird the development of pedagogy, especially in urban public schools, need to be examined. Indeed, public schools, as places where dominant American values are affirmed and reproduced, are also places where struggles for making meaning are most prominent. By critically reading the world, Black teenagers construct their identities through redefining what it is that constitutes respectable thinking and behaving in a racist society. In effect, they disrupt the discursive grid engendering values that, in this society, serve white supremacist ends. Specifically, these values range along a continuum where, at one end, control and conformity are most salient and, at the other, consensus and harmony are promoted.

Pedagogically speaking, public schools, for the most part, tend to be conservative places that employ educational practices where knowledge is transmitted from the teacher to the student. "Truth," in these cases, is treated as an absolute and unchanging entity. Envisioned this way, it is accessed by knowledge that is also absolute and unchanging and, further, that transcends time and circumstance. Brazilian educator Paulo Freire describes the dominant educational practice associated with this static view of truth—and by extension, knowledge and humanity—as the "banking method" of education. Here, "education becomes the act of depositing, in which students are the depositories and the teacher is the depositor" (1990, p. 58). This type of education emphasizes control, rigidity, and conformity. Hence, the banking method of education promotes *literacy for stupidification*, where education is reduced to "mindless, meaningless drills and exercises given 'in preparation for multiple choice exams and writing gobbledygook in imitation of the psycho-babble that surrounds them'" (Macedo, 1994, p. 16). Schools that employ these practices effectively function to sort out students in ways that reflect and reproduce oppressive economic and social realities in the larger society, thus revealing the political nature of schooling.

As in the case of conservative approaches to education, liberal schooling is most pronounced in the narrowly defined area of literacy. Here, emphasis is placed on the *process* of learning as opposed to the *product* of education. Yet, rarely do educators who emphasize the process of learning acknowledge the "culture of power" in which schools exist and in which teachers are situated (Delpit, 1995). In the absence of an interrogation of how schools serve to reproduce and affirm inequality in the United States, teachers fail to see how their most respectable and egalitarian actions may in fact "gradually incite rebelliousness on the part of children and adolescents" (Freire & Macedo, 1987, p. 121). Consequently, the notion of "failure" is inevitably projected onto adolescents of color rather than viewed as a social requirement intrinsic to a myopic view of what it means to be human, especially as it relates to being so in a hostile environment.

Both conservative and liberal pedagogical practices employed in public schools can be seen, then, to emerge as a dialectic between specific conceptions of truth and humanity. This interchange is realized in the way truth is pursued, or how knowledge is acquired, and is further informed by assumptions pertaining to the relationship between truth and human beings. When truth is believed to be objective, absolute, and external to the reality of human beings, as it is often conceived by those who function within conservative pedagogical frameworks, adolescents are viewed as automatons into which teachers deposit predetermined tidbits of knowledge. On the other hand, when truth is viewed to be relative to the experiences of the knower, teachers often reduce students to encapsulated, solipsist entities. Under these circumstances, students evince their understanding of truth by engaging in imaginative excursions that often undermine the egalitarian objectives of teachers who fail to acknowledge that some of our deepest preconceptions have been historically conditioned by the oppressive values of the wider society.

A critical reading of how truth and knowledge is conceived in the wider society, based on an interrogation of their underlying assumptions, is necessary to engage the powerful identities that Black teenagers bring to school. For teachers, this means re-evaluating the ideologies that frame dominant American pedagogical practices, especially as they relate to the values of conformity, control, consensus, and harmony. By acknowledging that these values may also negate self-determination and ethical resistance to oppression, educators better position themselves to understand that truth is simultaneously relative and absolute. Truth is relative owing to the multiple perspectives that individuals bring to bear on reading reality. It is absolute given the constraints that are requisite for living in a social context. In order to move beyond weak pedagogies that gloss over such complexities, teachers must address the possibility of teaching transgressively; that is, going against the grain to teach to transform our classrooms so that dominant truths reflect more broadly those multiple truths of the individuals that make up our classrooms—and society.

Footnote

1. During the fall of 1993, I conducted interviews with 20 Black female and male adolescents for a larger study (Duncan, 1994). Although their remarks, as recorded above, are somewhat decontextualized, they nonetheless provide insight into how these individuals negotiate both the conceptual and material symbolism of what it means to be Black in a white supremacist dominant culture. All names used in connection to the participants are pseudonyms.

References

Bakhtin, M. M. (1981). *The dialogic imagination: Four essays* (M. Holquist, Ed.; C. Emerson & M. Holquist, Trans.). Austin, TX: University of Texas.

Courts, P. (1991). *Literacy and empowerment: The meaning makers*. NY: Bergin & Garvey.

Delpit, L. (1995). *Other people's children: Cultural conflict in the classroom.* NY: The New Press.

Duncan, G. (1994). *The light before the dawn: Toward a critically grounded theory of Black consciousness, adolescent development, and schooling.* Doctoral dissertation, The Claremont Graduate School. Ann Arbor, MI: *University Microfilm International,* No. 9502329.

Freire, P. (1990). *Pedagogy of the oppressed.* NY: Continuum. (Original work published in 1970.)

_____. and Macedo, D. (1987). *Literacy: Reading the word and the world.* South Hadley, MA: Bergin & Garvey Publishers, Inc.

Gardner, H. (1983). *Frames of mind: The theory of multiple intelligences.* NY: Basic Books.

Harre, R. and Gillett, G. (1994). *The discursive mind.* Thousand Oaks, CA: Sage.

Kozol, J. (1986). *Illiterate America.* NY: Plume.

Macedo, D. (1994). *Literacies of power: What Americans are not allowed to know.* Boulder, CO: Westview Press.

Wertsch, J. (1991). *Voices of the mind: A sociocultural approach to mediated action.* Cambridge, MA: Harvard University Press.

TOWARDS MULTIPLE PERSPECTIVES ON LITERACY

Lil Thompson

I always begin with a quote—

> I saw tomorrow look at me through children's eyes
> And thought how carefully I'd teach,
> If only I were wise.

The 62nd Annual Claremont Reading Conference would be my twenty-second as a presenter. Over the years I have anticipated with great interest the title of the theme, and this was no exception. "Towards Multiple Perspectives on Literacy" would give me yet another opportunity to climb on to a favorite "band wagon." Perhaps, I thought, I should consult *Webster's 3rd New Dictionary* to get a definition of "literacy." What did it tell me? I quote, "Literacy—a state of being literate." Perhaps I should look up "literate" and found it was "the ability to read a short, simple passage and answer questions about it." Is that all I had to do to make children literate? I must get them to read and then check that they could answer questions? I did have painful memories of the primers I had to read as a child. After the joy of the story came those awful questions at the end. My teachers must have read *Webster's Dictionary*!

How different has been my philosophy as a teacher of children over the last fifty-five years. I looked at the children. I did want them to read and write, but I wanted so much more for them. I used to think that writing came first. Children not only scribble from a very early age but they can tell you "what it says." Professor Spencer would have us think that children "read" from birth onwards—that is that they "see" from experience, read what they "see": mother's face et cetera. Learning begins as soon as the child is born. Each day there are new things to observe which are experienced, learned, and stored for future use. Learning does not wait until the child starts school. The child educates itself and needs new experiences daily to help him/her develop into a literate adult.

Let us look at the child to see how language develops as it grows, before the reading/writing stage as we see it in school. I have stated "ad nauseam" that "language is central to the whole process of education" and that the early years are so important. So much research has gone into how language develops and even now new theories are put forward. It has been emphasized that a close relationship exists between language competence and cognitive development. Discussions about whether children get their language from genes or by imitation of their environment are never ending. Bernstein, as early as 1960, told us that children acquire most of their language, though not most of their vocabulary, by age four or five. Piaget saw language as being separate from thought. So many theories, but the general consensus has always been that the development of language abilities goes hand in hand with the development of mental ability.

Looking at the speech of a three-year-old who has never been told that to make the plural of a noun you add an "s," we are amazed that he can follow a grammatical rule he does not know exists so much that for sometime he will add an "s" to all nouns and say "look at the sheeps!" We do not tell that same child how to make a past tense of a verb but he will tell you "my dad builded a garage, he digged the garden and a bird flied over." We do know however, that we must foster language development in order to maximize the child's potential for both comprehension and expression; we must, as Dr. Mia Kelmer

Pringle stated "bathe the child in language from birth onwards. It enriches his growing mind."

Linguists have their theories to add to the confusion of those of us who teach and who have the "literacy goal" within our sights. Although we are fairly certain that imitation and reinforcement play an important role in the acquisition of early language ability, we still cannot explain what happens in the child's mind that enables it to generate original sentences he has never heard before. To me, after all my years in teaching children, it is still a mystery which fascinates me, and in my school it was important that a child should be encouraged to talk and listen. I did my own research and found that children of literate parents had a head start when they came to school. In the 1970's I was part of a team looking at the linguistically deprived children in a city called Norwich. These children were labeled at an early age as "backward." They were placed with similar children in a "bottom group" in the class. We found that often children from the same family would be "educationally subnormal." So, we looked at those families and found that they came from homes where there were no books and very little conversation, even between the parents. Often the parents would stray in to listen to the storyteller, and in time they would take time to read to their children. The marked improvement in their "bottom groupers" was remarkable. They came alive!

I have been described in the Claremont Reading Conference Program as a master teacher who realizes that children learn best when the classroom provides rich experiences for dramatic play, creative storytelling, and inspired fun. As a child myself I was taught that I had to "sit up" and "shut up" with my arms folded behind my back. The children in my school were encouraged to do just the opposite. Indeed, I had my goal of developing literacy, but I realized that this could be achieved by allowing them freedom of movement. There were not enough chairs in the classroom to seat all the children for I realized that in childhood there is perpetual motion; they find it difficult to stand still. As for "shutting up," they talk, not only to their peer group—but to themselves if there is no other listener! They practice their skill, not only to gossip but to put their thoughts into words. As teachers we have to be good listeners, for children love to communicate, and they can tell when teachers are interested in what they have to say.

The teacher in the classroom must create the fertile soil where children can have the opportunity to live through the real experience and to talk about what is happening while it is going on as well as after it has been completed. A rich environment is not enough; children develop language best when required to use words to express concepts and thoughts about what is happening. "Look at me," they will say "I can tell you all about it." If you are wise you listen—perhaps increasing the child's vocabulary at the same time.

My classroom, at all times, was a hive of activity. Using an "integrated day" approach, every area of the curriculum would be in evidence from basic to creative activities. The day would begin with the children sharing orally their news items and then recording in their journals their own individual items. Children writing and then reading their "news" was the foundation of all the narrative writing. As I shared their writing I would talk about grammar and spelling and all the "rules" that, if taken as a class lesson, would be of significance to only a few. The "one to one" discussion "eyeball to eyeball" would be suited to the child I was working with at the time. I would point out the use of interrogation, and exclamation marks, and the use of apostrophe and spelling rules. The date, weather, wind direction, and temperature would be recorded. This "habit" of writing daily made sure that children had to think. They then had to put their thoughts into writing. In time it became as automatic as cleaning their teeth! The ability to express adequately on paper should be practiced and refer to immediate experiences. There should be development of writing for pleasure as well as functional language, and communication through the written word should be for sheer enjoyment and should widen horizons and fulfill the whole personality.

Thus the journal writing laid the foundation for those imaginative stories which would be written in the Authors' Corner, an area enclosed, so that the children could go and write when the "spirit" moved. When children listen to stories and respond to them in creative ways, they are developing both receptive and expressive language processes. Literature acts as a language experience in both creative and communicate ways. The value of reading to children and having children read widely themselves has been discussed constantly. Many of our children come from homes where there are no books and very little or no storytelling. The teacher must promote attitudes—favorable ones—towards reading, extending backgrounds of experience, providing entertainment, and instilling an interest in books. These are the best reasons for sharing literature with children. Children's books are a rich source of language.

Did my children have those boring basals? Indeed, they did not! There were books everywhere. Books to look at and enjoy visually. Books to be read to them, books for them to read to themselves, their friends or their teacher. I reckon basals, ditto sheets, and testing were responsible for much of present day illiteracy. I wanted my children to read because they enjoyed it, not because they had to. "Come out you and read" must have destroyed many a reader. I quote from Dr. Malcolm Douglass, "There are other ways of inferring whether reading has occurred, if we need such. I suspect, however, that we are spending far too much time in these activities; it would be better to give children more time to read, rather than asking them, so often, to prove that they have read something. In simple words, reading is a very private behavior and must necessarily and thankfully remain so." Given a free choice from the book corner I found that children did not choose books that were too "easy" or too "hard," they chose books that held a special interest for them. Dan Fader in his "Hooked on Books" (which you all should read) told the story of Bill, a thirteen year old, second grade reader. Dan found him reading—or trying to read "Jaws," "Isn't that book hard?" Dan asked, "Sure it's hard, but it's worth it!" replied Bill. This was in contrast to a publication I had read which said "Every student is expected to pass a content test on each book. This way I make sure that the books have been read. My students learn about theme, characterization, imagery, et cetera." I added—"and to hate reading." A fog of content, tests, literacy terms, workbooks and skill sheets have obscured the vision and distracted thought. I agree with Bruno Bettelheim who said somewhere, "We should concentrate on awakening the will to read. We cheat the child of what it should gain from the experience of literature—a greater understanding of itself and others, and help in solving life's problems." John Dewey always inspired me. What did he say about literature? "A story that evokes laughter, wonder, sadness, curiosity or fear invites a reader to have a genuine interaction with the characters and the events in their lives."

I quote Tolkein, "Children's books, like their clothes, should allow for growth, and their books, at any rate, should encourage it."

I know from experience that imaginative literature, including science fiction and fantasy encourages growth in young readers.

Stories give us language and when a child listens to a good story he adds to the storehouse of words and phrases that it will use sometime, somewhere. Roald Dahl's books have surely inspired, not only children, but teachers. How can a teacher not be excited by and I quote from the *Enormous Crocodile*, "In the biggest, brownest, muddiest river in Africa two crocodiles lay with their heads just above the water. One of the crocodiles was enormous. The other was not so big." The listening child will have imagined those two crocodiles and even though the word "enormous" is a "new" word, they will deduce that one crocodile is big and the other not so big. The word "enormous" will be theirs forever. Think about it—we as teachers add daily to that "word store" in the brain. I have seen a child say over and over again a word which has "tickled its fancy," and later seen it used in context in a piece of writing. Memories from my childhood came back to me. Robert Louis Stevenson's picture is as vivid to me now as when I first heard it—

"Whenever the moon and stars are set,
Whenever the wind is high
All night long in the dark and wet
A man goes riding by.
Late in the night when the fires are out
Why does he gallop and gallop about?"

Words make another place and the imagination does the rest. The ways those words were read to me, the sense of the dramatic situation and character were laid down, as music is, as a rich bed of memories.

I quote again "The Plowden Report." "We are convinced of the value of stories for children, stories told to them, stories read to them and the stories they read for themselves. It is through story as well as through drama and other forms of creative work that children grope for the meaning of experiences that have already overtaken them, savour again their pleasures and reconcile themselves to their own inconsistencies and those of others. As they try on first one story book character and then another, imagination and sympathy, the power to enter into another personality and situation, which is a characteristic of childhood and a fundamental condition for good social relationships is preserved and nurtured. It is also through literature that children feel forward to the experiences, the hopes and fears that await them in adult life. It is almost certainly in childhood that children are most susceptible, both to living examples, and the examples they find in books. As children listen to stories, as they take books down from the library shelf, they may, as Graham Greene suggests in "The Lost Childhood," "be choosing their future and the values that will dominate it."

Teachers can weave spells with the story telling. I recently met a middle-aged lady who reminded me that I was once her teacher. "I hated needlework lessons," she said, "but you made us do it. It was only bearable because of those dramatic stories which you told us whilst we were sewing. You kept us spellbound, and do you know, I've told those same stories to my children and my grandchildren." "Outside a salty wind blows snow against the panes of the window. Foghorns are grumping far in the distance. The coal fire in the grate burns intense and silent. Then..." "What happens next?" the children will ask. "I know," says the imaginative one. "Just be quiet and let her get on. Go on Mrs. Thompson, what happens next?" And so I go on, and on, and on! Readers begin as listeners, dependent upon teachers and parents for initial access to literature that is well beyond what they can read comfortably and enjoyably by themselves. Listening skills if developed are two years ahead of reading skills.

So we bathe our children in stories. There has never been such a wealth of literature as there is today. However, a word of warning, if the teacher is not in love with good literature, there is less hope for the children in her charge. Stories offer us giants to grapple with, foxes to outwit, wrongs to be put right. That is how it should be. Often for children the focus is on action, and on feelings related to acting and suffering. Literature invites us to make an imaginary world, images from the printed words.

"Can we act it?" they will ask. Perhaps for me drama is the "open door" to literacy. Plowden reminds us that children love to "try on" one character after another. I am sure that the children in my class in Tulare will never forget *James and the Giant Peach* by Roald Dahl. They scripted the play, learned their parts without realizing it, built a set and made their costumes. As there was competition for the parts, they learned them all. Children who, until they had read this book, had shown little interest, came alive as grasshoppers and earthworms.
"Are there any more books by Roald Dahl?" they ask. High school children in Montebello fell in love with Shakespeare through the love story of Romeo and Juliet. I have memories of the scene in the tomb. No Hollywood actors died more feelingly than my Romeos!

"Here's to my love! O true apothecary. Thy drugs are quick. Thus with a kiss I die."
No actresses died more courageously than my Juliets!
"Oh happy dagger. This is thy sheath; there rest and let me die."
The witches scenes in Macbeth were committed to memory forever.

"Fair is foul, and foul is fair.:
Hover through the fog and filthy air."

Sympathy for Hamlet as he says"

"The time is out of joint, Oh cursed spite that I was ever born, To set it right."

These plays of Shakespeare are literature woven from the fabric of life, and children respond to its difficulties, tragedies, and joys because, as young as they are, they are human.

Drama is an important perspective of literacy. Children gain confidence in speaking; their speech improves. They develop fluency and benefit by having an increased vocabulary. There is a development and expression of ideas with an increased ability to communicate with people. Spoken language acts as a stimulus for writing. There is an improvement in listening skills and an awareness of language in different situations.

Recently I found in an antique bookshop a *Journal of Education* published in 1911. On the front page there was an advertisement for some books called *Speaking and Writing*, written by William Maxwell, City Superintendent of Schools, New York; Emma Johnston, Principal of Brooklyn Training School for Teachers; and Madalene Barnum, a teacher of English at the same school. The blurb states, "The books make the study of oral English as systematic as the study of written English. The series teaches the delightful art of oral story telling by furnishing stories for reproduction, with numerous suggestions and directions. The work in dramatization develops the child's powers of imagination and expression." Bilingual education was not forgotten! "These books are of particular value to children of foreign parentage." So in 1911 some were moving towards literacy in education. In 1994 I picked up a Central Coast Literacy Council leaflet which stated that 17,000 adults in Northern Santa Barbara County can't read warning labels on bottles and cans, read freeway and street signs, understand messages, fill out application forms, use a cheque book, read newspapers, and take their rightful place as citizens. How and were did we fail as teachers?

Do these statistics tell us that we need other perspectives on literacy? When I began as a teacher in 1940 I was full of enthusiasm. I would have felt professionally inadequate if those 50+ children in my class left unable to read and write. I raised my voice many times against the number of hours children spent in front of a television screen, and just as I thought I was winning along came the videos and computers! There would be some educators who would challenge me on this issue. I read advertisements about "Tapping into Technology." I quote, "Help your student build their seven different kinds of smart, try these computer software programs." The claims to make a student "word smart" are backed by a program which includes 8,000 original story starters. Certainly I cannot compete with that claim! I must admit that children have a natural attraction to computers, so getting them to spend time in front of a monitor is not very hard. The challenge is to make sure the time children spend interacting with technology is constructive and not a mere extension of a video game arcade. The computer should not be a new kind of "babysitter." The enthusiastic teacher must not be in competition, for the good teacher knows that to reach all students he/she has to design lessons that address all the perspectives of learning—auditory, visual, and kinetic. A good book can satisfy; you can't take a computer to bed—but you can a book.

A leaflet from the American Association of University Women says it all for me. "The definition of literacy has changed from being able to just read and write to the multiple literacies needed to communicate in our fast changing world. Working with schools, librarians, educators, and business leaders we can create opportunities that will meet the needs of literacy for the future." My perspective has always been to create an environment where the children in my school want to read and write, not because I say so, but because they are excited about learning. The early years are so very important; life is fun, and we, as teachers, by our enthusiasm, must share that joy with them by encouraging them to talk, listen, write, and read. If we provide the fertile soil, they will surely grow into literate human beings. We must help every child to go forth with confidence and vitality. We must help every child attain its potential. We must prepare the child to take its place in the world of today—not yesterday.

READ ACROSS AMERICA: CELEBRATING AMERICA WITH BOOKS TO READ ALOUD

Carolyn R. Angus

"Read Across America," the theme for the 75th anniversary of Children's Book Week, can be used to develop a read-aloud celebration of our country's diversity. A good place to start is with one of the recently published anthologies that celebrate America through poetry and art. These include *Hand in Hand* (1994), edited by Lee Bennett Hopkins; *Celebrate America in Poetry and Art* (1994), edited by Nora Panzer; *Singing America* (1995), edited by Neil Philip; and *Celebrating America* (1994), edited by Laura Whipple. *From Sea to Shining Sea* (1993), edited by Amy L. Cohn, is an extensive collection of American folklore: folk tales, folk songs, poems, and essays. All of these collections serve as rich sources of read-aloud fare.

A variety of interpretations of the theme "Read Across America" is possible. Books can be read that chronicle journeys made by many people, such as those of slaves on the Underground Railroad or of pioneers moving westward over the Oregon Trail. Other books cover journeys recorded in personal journals and diaries, such as Jim Murphy's *Into the Deep Forest with Henry David Thoreau* (1995), a record of a canoe trip through the Maine wilderness, and Paul Fleischman's *Townsend's Warbler* (1992), based on naturalist John Townsend's journal record of a trip along the Oregon Trail in 1834.

Another possibility is to read books that focus on a particular region, such as the prairie, a specific geographic feature, such as the Florida Everglades, or a state. Here as an example, a variety of books set in Maine is featured. A year-long challenge would be to read a book for each state.

Reading about the plants and animals of an area as well as its history and folklore gives depth to our understanding. Barbara Bash's *Ancient Ones* (1994), for example, presents the life cycle of the Douglas fir and the story of the old-growth forests of the Pacific Northwest. In *Wolves* (1993), Seymour Simon considers the biology of wolves, myths about them, and the conservationists' efforts to preserve this "symbol of the wilderness."

The inclusion of historical and contemporary fiction about the ties between people and places completes this celebration of America. Patricia MacLachlan's *Skylark* (1994) and Mildred D. Taylor's *The Well* (1995) are representative of short novels with a strong sense of place that read aloud well.

The following sample of recently published picture books, novels, folklore, poetry, and non-fiction that make great read- alouds is offered as an invitation to join in the celebration of people and places in America.

Appelt, K. (1995). *Bayou Lullaby*. Illus. by Neil Waldman. New York, NY: Morrow. Appelt enriches her lullaby song to a "bayou gal" with the rhythms of Cajun speech. Bold images of the bayou at night are presented in Waldman's brilliantly double-page acrylic paintings done on a black background. (picture book)

Bash, B. (1994). *Ancient Ones: The World of the Old-Growth Douglas Fir*. San Francisco, CA: Sierra Club. Author-artist Bash pairs a lyrical text with dramatic double-page watercolor paintings to present the life cycle of the Douglas fir and the story of the old-growth forests of the Pacific Northwest. (non-fiction)

Bates, K.L. (1993). *America the Beautiful.* Illus. by Neil Waldman. New York, NY: Atheneum. Waldman's majestic landscape paintings of scenes from coast to coast—the Napa Valley, the Great Plains, Niagara Falls, and 12 other panoramic views—depict the diverse beauty of America that is celebrated in Bates' poem (first published in 1893 and later set to the music of Samuel A. Ward, becoming a favorite patriotic song). (poetry)

Bial, R. (1995). *The Underground Railroad.* Boston, MA: Houghton. By pairing an interesting, informative text with color photographs that he took on visits to stations along the Underground Railroad and prints of archival documents, Bial gives readers a real sense of these important stops along the route to freedom taken by thousands of slaves in the years before the Civil War. (non-fiction)

Blackstone, M. (1995). *This is Maine.* Illus. by John Segal. New York, NY: Holt. Just a few short sentences and simple, well-composed watercolor paintings capture those special features of Maine that lead Mainers to say that "Maine is the only place." (picture book)

Boulton, J. (1994). *Only Opal: The Diary of a Young Girl.* Illus. by Barbara Cooney. New York, NY: Philomel. Boulton's adaptation of the diary of Opal Whitely (written at the turn of the century when she was five and six) tells the story of an orphan taken in by an Oregon family. Opal is burdened with chores, done dutifully, although she longs to be free to spend more time exploring the world around her. The young girl's joyous spirit in spite of hardships is communicated in the lyrical text and Cooney's fresh watercolor paintings. (picture book)

Brandenburg, J. (1995). *An American Safari: Adventures on the North American Prairie.* New York, NY: Walker. With stunning color photographs and an engaging text, Brandenburg tells the story of his attachment to the American prairie through a lifetime of exploration and photography. He also offers an eloquent plea for the preservation and restoration of this special American landscape. (non-fiction)

Bravo, O. (1995). *Olga's Cup and Saucer: A Picture Book with Recipes.* New York, NY: Holt. From June through September, Nickel Penny Rooster supplies the baker with fresh fruits and vegetables. Her goal: to help in the kitchen. And she does—if only accidentally—and creates a new treat, Fresh Raspberry Pizza. Five original recipes by Olga Bravo, the owner of the real "Olga's Cup and Saucer" in Little Compton, Rhode Island, are included. (picture book)

Clark, M. G. (1995). *The Threatened Florida Black Bear.* New York, NY: Cobblehill. In telling the story of Florida's black bear, Clark uses real-life incidents. The result is an information book that reads like an adventure story.

Cohn, Amy L. (Ed.). (1993). *From Sea to Shining Sea: A Treasury of American Folklore and Folk Songs.* Illus. by Caldecott Medal and Honor Book Artists. New York, NY: Scholastic. The diversity of America is reflected in this collection of over 140 folktales, folk songs, poems, and essays. The selections are grouped by historical period and gloriously illustrated by Caldecott artists. This rich resource of America's folklore and history includes extensive source notes. (folklore)
Connelly, B. (1993). *Follow the Drinking Gourd.* One cassette. Read by Morgan Freeman. Boston, MA: Rabbit Ears. This story of an Alabama slave family's escape to freedom on the Underground Railroad is given a dramatic reading by Morgan

Freeman. He effectively transports listeners to the river bank
along which the family travels northward and makes them feel
the dangers of the journey. Taj Mahal provides vocal and
instrumental accompaniment, using vintage instruments which
add an authentic tone. Side two consists of more of Taj Mahal's
bluesy tunes, which will echo in listeners' memories as will the
voice of Freeman telling Connelly's story based on the
traditional folk song "Follow the Drinking Gourd." (audio book)

Cooper, M. L. (1995). *Bound for the Promised Land: The
Great Black Migration.* New York, NY: Lodestar. Cooper
chronicles the experiences of the men, women, and children who
were part of "the Great Migration" from 1915 to 1930 of black
Southerners who sought the promise of a better life in the
industrial cities of the Northeast and Midwest. The accounts of
the creation of large black neighborhoods such as Chicago's
South Side and New York City's Harlem are particularly
interesting. (non-fiction)

Creech, S. (1994). *Walk Two Moons.* New York, NY:
HarperCollins. Thirteen-year-old Salamanca Tree Hiddle
journeys from Ohio to Idaho with her grandparents, retracing the
route her mother took one April morning when she left home and
never returned, in spite of her promise to be back before the
tulips bloomed. The 1995 Newbery Medal book. (fiction)

Douglas, W. O. (1994). *Muir of the Mountains.* Illus. by Daniel
San Souci. San Francisco, CA: Sierra Club. Douglas'
biography (originally published in 1964) of John Muir, pioneer
conservationist and founder of the Sierra Club, has been reissued
in a slightly abridged form and with new drawings by San Souci.
Douglas makes extensive use of quotations from John Muir's
own writings, giving a strong sense of Muir's adventurous spirit
and deep love of the natural world. (biography)

Esbensen, B. J. (1994). *The Great Buffalo Race: A Seneca Tale*. Illus. by Helen K. Davie. Boston, MA: Little, Brown. Esbensen retells the Seneca legend of how the buffalo got its hump. Davie uses rich earth tones and incorporates Iroquois patterns in her stunning watercolor illustrations. (folklore)

Fleischman, P. (1992). *Townsend's Warbler*. New York, NY: HarperCollins. Using excerpts from Townsend's original journal and black-and-white illustrations of paintings from the period, Fleischman interweaves accounts of the journey of naturalist John Townsend along the Oregon Trail in 1834 and the migratory trek of the bird that bears his name. (non-fiction)

Geisert, B. and A. Geisert. (1995). *Haystack*. Boston, MA: Houghton. The brief informative text and striking colored etchings of this picture book documentary pay tribute to the huge haystacks that were once familiar sights on the working farms that dotted the prairie landscape. (picture book)

George, J. C. (1995). *Everglades*. Illus. by Wendell Minor. New York, NY: HarperCollins. "My story will be different from any you have heard, because this river is like no other river on Earth. There is only one Everglades." So begins the storyteller's tale of the history of this unique ecosystem—from origin to imminent destruction—which ends on a note of hope. The plant and animal symbols of the vanishing Everglades flourish in Minor's beautiful paintings. (non-fiction)

Giovanni, N. (1994). *Knoxville, Tennessee*. Illus. by Larry Johnson. New York, NY: Scholastic. Johnson's richly colored paintings reflect the warmth and joy of Giovanni's poem in which she shares memories of summers spent with her grandparents in Knoxville. (poetry)

Hamilton, V. (1993). *Many Thousand Gone: African Americans from Slavery to Freedom.* Illus. by Leo Dillon and Diane Dillon. New York, NY: Knopf. This history of slavery in America—from the earliest days of slave trading to the Emancipation Proclamation—is as readable as it is informative. The Dillons' add striking images of the individuals profiled in the text. (non-fiction)

Haskins, J. (1993). *Get on Board: The Story of the Underground Railroad.* New York, NY: Scholastic. Haskins includes the stories of courageous conductors, stationmasters, and passengers in his well-research history of the Underground Railroad. (non-fiction)

Hopkins, L. B. (Ed.). (1994). *Hand in Hand: An American History Through Poetry.* Illus. by Peter M. Fiore. New York, NY: Simon & Schuster. Hopkins has chosen over 75 poems by Walt Whitman, Langston Hughes, Carl Sandburg, Gwendolyn Brooks, and other poets for this history of the United States—from the landing of the Pilgrims in 1620 to America's voyages into space—through poetry. (poetry)

Hyatt, P. R. (1995). *Coast to Coast with Alice.* Minneapolis, MN: Carolrhoda. The journal entries of 16-year-old Minna Jahns tell the story of the cross-country auto trip from Hackensack, New Jersey, to San Francisco, California, she took with neighborhood friend Alice Ramsey in 1909. The fictional journal is based on the memoirs of Alice Ramsey; photographs of the actual journal are included. (fiction)

Jouris, D. (1994). *All Over the Map: An Extraordinary Atlas of the United States.* Berkeley, CA: Ten Speed. This collection of thematic maps—a literary map, a mythical map, an edible map, and 30 more—that feature towns that actually exist is informative as well as entertaining. (non-fiction)

Karl, J. (1994). *America Alive: A History.* Illus. by Ian Schoenherr. New York, NY: Philomel. In the foreword, Karl says that *America Alive* is "a personal history; it is history as I see it" and acknowledges that it is a selective one. Herein lies the strength of *America Alive* as a history of the United States: vivid images of people, places, and events are offered in a format that is engaging and accessible to young people. (non-fiction)

Kessler, B. (1993). *John Henry.* One cassette. Read by Denzel Washington. Boston, MA: Rabbit Ears. Denzel Washington tells the "guaranteed, gold-plated, 99.9 percent truth" about the legendary African-American hero John Henry; legendary blues artist B.B. King provides vocal and instrumental accompaniment. Washington draws listeners in, making them a part of the crowd that witnessed John Henry's victory over the steam drill in the famous steel-driving competition. On side two the music of B.B. King continues the celebration of the life of the larger-than-life hero John Henry. (non-fiction)

Knight, A. S. (1993). *The Way West: Journal of a Pioneer Woman.* Adapted by Lillian Schlissel. Illus. by Michael McCurdy. New York, NY: Simon & Schuster. The dated entries of Amelia Stewart Knight's diary give readers a sense of the hardships she, her husband, and seven children endured on their 1853 journey from Iowa to the Oregon Territory. (non-fiction)

Kroll, S. (1994). *By the Dawn's Early Light: The Story of The Star Spangled Banner.* Illus. by Dan Andreasen. New York, NY: Scholastic. Kroll's dramatic narrative and Andreasen's exquisite oil paintings provide an engaging, historically accurate account of the writing of "The Star Spangled Banner" by Francis Scott Key in 1814. The author's note includes a photograph of the original manuscript of the poem, a musical arrangement, and maps. (poetry)

Kroll, S. (1994). *Lewis and Clark: Explorers of the American West.* Illus. by Richard Williams. New York, NY: Holiday House. Kroll gives a brief account of the 1804-1806 expedition of Meriwether Lewis and William Clark up the Missouri River and across to the Pacific Ocean. (non-fiction)

Krull, K. (Ed.). (1992). *Gonna Sing My Head Off!": American Folk Songs for Children.* Illus. by Allen Garns. New York, NY: Knopf. This treasury of 62 folk songs includes cowboy songs, patriotic songs, lullabies, protest songs, sea chanties, camp songs, spirituals, work songs, and more. The songs are accompanied by simple musical arrangements for piano and guitar, historical headnotes and exuberant, colorful illustrations. (folklore)

Krupinski, L. (1994). *A New England Scrapbook: A Journey Through Poetry, Prose, and Pictures.* New York, NY: HarperCollins. Beautiful paintings (a cranberry bog in North Falmouth, Massachusetts; Nibble Light, Cape Neddick, Maine; a farm house in Wilton, New Hampshire, and other scenes), brief descriptive passages, and poems by American poets invite young readers to explore the New England region. (poetry)

Lawrence, J. (1993). *The Great Migration: An American Story.* New York, NY: HarperCollins. Lawrence's series of 60 panels painted in 1940 and 1941 (from collections of The Museum of Modern Art, New York, and The Phillips Collection, Washington, D.C.) and his accompanying narrative chronicle the exodus of African Americans from the rural South around the time of World War I as they moved north seeking better lives in industrial cities. "Migration," a poem by Walter Dean Myers in response to Lawrence's series of paintings, is appended. (non-fiction)

Lyons, M. E. (1995). *The Butter Tree: Tales of Bruh Rabbit.* Illus. by Mireille Vautier. New York, NY: Holt. Lyons retells six Bruh Rabbit stories collected between 1935 and 1941 in Beaufort County and Murrells Inlet, South Carolina, using language that makes these animal tales accessible to first readers. (folklore)

MacLachlan, P. (1994). *Skylark.* New York, NY: HarperCollins. In this sequel to the Newbery Medal book *Sarah, Plain and Tall,* the stress of drought leads Sarah to take her two stepchildren, Anna and Caleb, back to Maine to visit her aunts. Having left their father, Jacob, behind on their prairie farm, young Anna worries that they may never be a family again. (fiction)

Maestro, M. and Maestro, G. (1994). *Riddle City, USA!: A Book of Geography Riddles.* New York, NY: HarperCollins. The Maestros offer up a collection of over 50 original riddles about places—cities, states, rivers, mountains, parks, and famous sites—in the United States. (non-fiction)

McDermott, G. (1994). *Coyote: A Trickster Tale from the American Southwest.* New York, NY: Harcourt. Tired of trickster Coyote's bragging, the crows decide to teach him a lesson. McDermott incorporates Zuni folk art into his brightly colored illustrations, featuring a magnificent blue Coyote. (folklore)

Monjo, F.N. (1993). *The Drinking Gourd: A Story of the Underground Railroad.* Illus. by Fred Brenner. New York, NY: HarperCollins. Young Tommy Fuller and his father help a family of slaves escape to freedom on the Underground Railroad in this newly illustrated I Can Read edition of Monjo's adventure story based on the poem "Follow the Drinking Gourd." (fiction)

Murphy, J. (1993). *Across America on an Emigrant Train.* New York, NY: Clarion. Drawing heavily from Stevenson's own writings, Murphy gives a vivid account of Robert Louis Stevenson's 1879 journey by train across America with other emigrants. At the same time, Murphy provides a history of the transcontinental railroad. Archival photographs, engravings, and lithographs are included. (non-fiction)

Murphy, J. (1995). *Into the Deep Forest with Henry David Thoreau.* Illus. by Kate Kiesler. New York, NY: Clarion. Using excerpts from Thoreau's own journal, Murphy takes readers on a canoe trip through the Maine wilderness with Thoreau and two companions. Kiesler's oil paintings and pencil drawings reflect details of Thoreau's journal entries about his observations of nature and communicate a sense of adventure "in the deep forest." (non-fiction)

Panzer, N. (Ed.). (1994). *Celebrate America in Poetry and Art.* New York, NY: Hyperion. In the preface, Panzer says, "By paying visual and poetic tribute to the shared experience of the American people, past and present, this book celebrates America." This collection of American poetry and paintings, sculpture, drawings, photographs, and other works of art from the National Museum of American Art does just that. Biographical notes on the writers and artists are appended. (poetry)

Patent, D. H. (1995). *Return of the Wolf.* Illus. by Jared Taylor Williams. New York, NY: Clarion. Sedra, a young female wolf driven from her pack, meets a young male wolf and together they establish a territory and begin a new wolf pack with the birth of their pups in the spring. Told from the wolf's point of view, *Return of the Wolf* is a fascinating animal adventure story. (fiction)

Philip, N. (Ed.). (1995). *Singing America: Poems that Define a Nation.* Illus. by Michael McCurdy. New York, NY: Viking. For this extensive anthology, Philip has selected the works of American poets who have addressed the question, "What is America, what should it be, and what is it to me?" These "poems that define a nation" offer a rich history of America from different viewpoints. (poetry)

Ruby, L. (1994). *Steal Away Home.* New York, NY: Macmillan. Ruby tells the parallel stories of a Quaker family whose Lawrence, Kansas, home was a station on the Underground Railroad in the 1850s and twelve-year-old Dana Shannon, who discovers the skeleton of a black woman in a hidden room of the same house, which her family is restoring over 150 years later. (fiction)

Shannon, G. (1993). *Climbing Kansas Mountains.* Illus. by Thomas Allen. New York, NY: Bradbury. A young boy and his father get a bird's-eye view of the flat countryside when they climb to the top of a grain elevator—a "Kansas mountain." (picture book)

Simon, S. (1994). *Winter Across America.* New York, NY: Hyperion. Simon takes the reader on a wintertime journey across America with a lively text that considers the importance of the cold season in the cycle of life and exquisite color photographs that express the beauty of America in winter. Also *Autumn Across America* (1993). (non-fiction)

Simon, S. (1993). *Wolves.* New York, NY: HarperCollins. Simon considers the physical characteristics, habits, and natural environment of wolves, myths about wolves, and conservationists' efforts to preserve this "symbol of the wilderness" in a photoessay that has stunning color photographs of wolves in their natural habitat. (non-fiction)

Smith, M. (1995). *Counting our Way to Maine.* New York, NY: Orchard. A family counts from one baby to twenty fireflies on their summer vacation trip to Maine. Young children will also enjoy counting objects—eight mountains, fourteen buoys, nineteen clams, and so on—in the warmly humorous watercolor illustrations. (picture book)

Stanley, J. (1994). *I am an American: A True Story of Japanese Internment.* New York, NY: Macmillan. Stanley tells of the experiences of Shi Nomura, a high school student of Japanese ancestry and one of the more than 120,000 Americans imprisoned by the federal government following the Japanese attack on Pearl Harbor in 1941. In doing so, he also tells the larger story of Japanese internment during World War II. Black-and-white photographs from the collection of Shi Nomura, the National Archives, and other collections add to the impact of Stanley's account of life in the Manzanar relocation camp. (non-fiction)

Taylor, M. D. (1995). *The Well.* New York, NY: Dial. In this short novel set in the early 1900s in Mississippi, ten-year-old David narrates the story of an incident in which the Logan family shares its well water with both black and white neighbors whose wells have gone dry during a drought. *The Well* is just as compelling a story as Taylor's earlier books about the Logans. (fiction)

Whipple, L. (Ed.). (1994). *Celebrating America: A Collection of Poems and Images of the American Spirit.* New York, NY: Philomel. Whipple has selected poems by Carl Sandburg, Nikki Giovanni, Langston Hughes, Eve Merriam, Walt Whitman, and many other American poets and works of art from the Art Institute of Chicago, juxtaposing these verbal and visual images to celebrate America. (poetry)

Winter, J. (1995). *Cowboy Charlie.* New York, NY: Harcourt. *Cowboy Charlie* is the story of a young boy's dream of going west come true. This picture book biography is a tribute to the courage and spirit of Charles Marion Russell (1864-1926), who not only became a cowboy, but also one of the great American painters of the Wild West. (biography)

Wright, C. C. (1994). *Journey to Freedom: A Story of the Underground Railroad.* Illus. by Gershom Griffith. New York, NY: Holiday House. Eight-year-old Joshua chronicles the 20-day journey his family, runaway slaves from a Kentucky tobacco plantation, takes to freedom in Canada with conductor Harriet Tubman. An author's note provides brief historical information about the Underground Railroad of the mid-1800s; a map shows the journey of Joshua's family from Lexington, Kentucky to Ontario, Canada. (picture book)

Yep, L. (1993). *The Rainbow People.* Three cassettes. Read by George Guidall. New York, NY: Recorded Books. The 20 folk stories in this collection were adapted by Yep from tales originally recorded in a 1930s WPA oral history project in Oakland's Chinatown. The stories are grouped in five sections: Tricksters, Fools, Virtues and Vices, In Chinese America, and

Love. Guidall's reading is superb. He fully captures the mood of each story whether it is ghoulish, witty, ghostly, suspenseful, or even terrifying. The reading of Yep's introductory remarks for the book (Harper & Row, 1989) adds interesting cultural information. (audio book)

IF OSCAR THE GROUCH ONLY HAS EIGHT FINGERS, HOW CAN HE COUNT TO TEN? LANGUAGE, LITERACY, AND THE DEVELOPMENT OF MATHEMATICAL THOUGHT

Martin Bonsangue
Nancy Bonsangue
Janet Sharp

Abstract

Since language is the common vehicle from which literary symbols and mathematical thought are constructed, language-generated bridges between the two domains can strengthen a person's understanding of mathematics. This paper explores the role of language in the development and expression of mathematical concepts in certain non-Western cultures.[1]

Introduction

In early childhood we learn to count in this way: *one, two, three, four, five, six, seven, eight, nine, ten.* If we are counting on our fingers, we have just run out of fingers, and need to have some way of accounting for this fact. Of course, this is not hard to do, since we have the words for the numbers that follow ten: *eleven, twelve, thirteen, fourteen, fifteen, sixteen, seventeen, eighteen, nineteen, twenty.*

After the first two terms (*eleven and twelve*), the number words fall into a nice, predictable pattern: three-and-ten (shortened to *thirteen* for ease of speech), four-and-ten, five-and-ten (again shortened), and so on. After this, the pattern is repeated into the twenties (*twenty* is a contraction of two-tens), thirties, and beyond. Clearly our number words describe a system that is based on repeated countings of the fingers on both hands which we call a base ten numeration system. That is, the numbers are based on a complete set of ten fingers.

The Base Ten Number System

Since the number words are a bit tedious to write, we use other symbols, or numerals, to represent them. Children learn the digits to represent the numbers one through nine also at an early age: *1, 2, 3, 4, 5, 6, 7, 8, 9*.

But what do we write after *9*? Since the next finger makes one complete set of hands, we use a two-digit number to represent the completed set, namely, *10*, which indicates one complete set (of ten fingers) with none left over. A bit of reflection will show that we have no single digit to represent the number *ten*. Indeed, it is the necessity of a two-digit numeral to represent *ten* that characterizes our written base-ten numeration system.

After this, the numeral pattern is even easier to write than the word pattern is to say: *11 (one set of ten with one left over), 12 (one set of ten with two left over),* and so on with *13, 14, 15, 16, 17, 18, 19*. The idea that two complete sets of hands have been counted results in the numeral *20*.

Of course, it is easy to generate larger numbers. After counting *93, 94, 95, 96, 97, 98, 99* we need a new digit to represent one hundred, or one set of ten tens (imagine a set of hands in which each finger itself represents a set of hands). Thus, we logically follow the largest two-digit number *99* with the smallest three digit number *100*. Although the numbers are still in sequence, the extra digit was again necessary to accommodate the number of fingers on our hands. Likewise, after 999 we write 1,000, denoting a set of hands in which each finger represents 100. Scientists often write these "powers of ten" in exponential or scientific notation: $1,000 = 10^3$; $10,000 = 10^4$, etc. This notation is especially helpful since both language and experience eventually fail for naming large powers of ten, such as numbers of the magnitude 10^9 (world population), 10^{12} (the national debt), or 10^{23} (number of atoms in a chemical unit of measurement called a mole). Scientists have invented some *ad hoc* names to describe unusually large numbers, such as a googleplex (one followed by one hundred zeros). No matter how large the number, its expression is based on the assumption that the counter has ten fingers.

Number Systems Not Based on Ten

Oscar the Grouch's World

But what about a world where the hands are not formed like our own? Although almost any cartoon or funny paper character illustrates this, consider the fictitious, though not unimportant, world of Oscar the Grouch. Oscar, like most of the *Sesame Street* characters, has four fingers on each hand (Allen, 1990; CTW, 1991). Thus Oscar might count something like this: *1, 2, 3, 4, 5, 6, 7.* But what comes after *seven*? The next finger would make a complete set of hands so that he would write 10, or "one-zero," meaning one complete set of Grouch hands with no fingers left over. Thus, Oscar's counting scheme depends on his experience of *eight* fingers making one complete set. Of course,

Oscar has no single numeral for *eight* any more than we have one for *ten* (and, of course, our words *eight* and *nine* would have little meaning for Oscar, and the digits 8 and 9 would have no meaning). He would then continue to count *11, 12, 13, 14, 15, 16, 17, 20,* with the last number indicating his having completed two sets of Grouch hands.[2]

Of course, Oscar is just as capable of counting large numbers as we are. For example, if he were counting pieces of trash (Grouches love trash!) and reading off his tally marks, he would count as follows: *65, 66, 67, 70, 71, 72, 73, 74, 75, 76, 77.* The next piece of trash would be very significant for Oscar, since *77* is the largest two-digit number in his world. The next piece of trash would correspond to a complete set of Grouch hands in which each finger itself represents a set of hands. Thus, he would follow *77* with the numeral *100* (or "one-zero-zero"). Oscar would then be able to repeat the counting pattern *101, 102,* etc., up to his largest three-digit number, which is *777,* and would follow this with *1000.*

Keep in mind that we and Oscar can certainly refer to the same physical amounts although our references may appear to be quite different. For example, if we were counting a set of twenty-six pennies, we would say that there are *26,* that is, two sets of ten and six single pennies. Oscar, grouping the pennies in (what we would call) eights, would declare that there are *32* pennies, that is, three groups of eight plus two more. If we wrote numerals to represent the amount of money, we would assert that we have *26* cents, while Oscar would write that he has *32* cents. Although this difference in expression may seem trivial, consider the gap as the numbers grow. A new piece of furniture might cost us $600, while Oscar would say that he paid $1,122 (that is, 2 plus 2 eights plus 1 sixty-four plus 1 five hundred twelve); a new car might cost us $12,000, while Oscar would pay $27,340;

and our $300,000 house would cost poor Oscar more than a million Grouch dollars.

In all of these examples the quantity of pennies (or dollars) used in a transaction remains constant. It is the language and experience that we and Oscar bring to describe this amount that varies. Indeed, anyone who has briefly visited foreign countries and had to exchange money has had experiences similar to Oscar's, especially if he or she were in a country that used currency that was vastly different from his or her own.

Math on Ceres

Before leaving fictitious worlds to discuss the effects of mathematics and language in real ones, consider the story below (which we got from Rick Luttmann at Sonoma State University, who has designed and teaches a delightful course entitled "Ethnomathematics"). Can you figure out the answer to the questions? What other interesting questions could be posed?

I recently received the following letter from a friend of mine who flies to Saturn for his Christmas vacations:

'As I was rocketing past the asteroid Ceres, I saw a sign reading,'

White Star Diner
We Never Close
Easy Return to Spaceway
Catering to Travelers from All 13 Planets

'I knew there are only 9 planets, but I attributed this error to the eccentricity of some Cerean sign painter. But inside the diner was another sign that further perplexed me. It said,

Seating Capacity 134

'Yet as I looked around I could count only 58 chairs. The mystery was resolved for me when the waitress brought the menu, and I noticed her hands.'

1. How many fingers do you think the waitress had on each hand?

2. Why did the numbering of items on the menu skip from 5 to 10?

3. Suppose my friend was presented a bill for his meal of 351 New Cosmic Clams. How many—in our terms—would he have to pay?

4. The waitress, who didn't travel much, asked my friend how far it was to Saturn. He knew that it was 383 light-minutes away. What would he have to tell her so that she would understand correctly?"

Language and Mathematics

We have spent a few minutes exploring the worlds of Sesame Street and Ceres to better understand the relationship between mathematical thought and experience. In this section we will explore how language can serve as a clue to understanding this relationship within the context of various real life cultures.

John Ellis writes in his book *Language, Thought, and Logic* (1993) that,

A language is a unique, highly complex, ordered conceptual system. It is the most central factor in the social life of those who share it, and it is the most crucial thing that differentiates one community from another (p. 119).

In the discussion so far, we have talked about number symbols and number words, with some attention given to the origins of the number words themselves, such as four-and-ten for *fourteen*.[3] If we take Ellis' view to heart that language is central to the social life of a community and that differences in languages relate to differences between communities, then the mathematical language of a particular culture will reflect the values and experiences of that culture. Oscar the Grouch and the waitress on Ceres show how quantities might be expressed given the physical characteristics of the individual doing the counting. Aside from physical characteristics, however, Oscar and the waitress seem to have much in common with you and me in that they speak English and live in societies structured much like ours.[4]

However, the issues that Oscar and the Cerean waitress raise in terms of mathematics as a cultural enterprise are critical in understanding the role that language plays in the development of mathematics in both western and non-western cultures. To see this, the discussion now turns to the mathematics of hunter/ gatherer societies as distinguished from agricultural/ industrial societies. As outlined in Table 1, hunter/gatherer societies are self-contained and alter themselves to fit into the environment, while agricultural/industrial societies are inter-dependent and alter the environment to meet the society's needs. In hunter/ gatherer societies jobs are centralized rather than specialized with human energy rather than non-human energy used to accomplish tasks. As we shall see, in hunter/gatherer societies mathematical expression emerges from experience and context, whereas in agricultural/industrial societies mathematical expression tends to be devoid of context with the emphasis placed on isolating specific parts rather than on valuing the whole.

Table 1
Characteristics of Hunter/Gatherer and Agricultural/Industrial Societies

Hunter/Gatherer Societies	Agricultural/Industrial Societies
Self-contained	Interdependent
Societies are altered to adapt to the environment	Environment is altered to meet society's needs
All adults do all jobs—no technology	Specialization of jobs; use of technology
Human energy used to accomplish tasks	Machines and domesticated animals used to accomplish tasks
Handcrafts—every item different	Machine crafts—every item identical
Mathematical expression emerges from experience and context	Attempt to isolate variables and remove context in mathematical expression

Source: Adapted from Beeler, 1990, and Denny, 1990.

The remainder of the paper discusses four aspects of mathematical life in some non-Western cultures: counting systems, arithmetic operations, geometry, and measurement, using an outline described by Denny (1990). The last section discusses the role that culture and experience plays, not only in understanding how mathematical thought and language are developed, but how this process defines into discrete categories those things that are and are not valued by the society in which that experience occurs.

Non-Western Counting Systems

Chumash Number System

Madison Beeler (1990) did extensive research regarding the family of languages called Chumash spoken along the coast of southern California in aboriginal times. Beeler writes that the counting systems used in the various Chumash dialects depended on four basic root words and that the number *four* held special significance in the system. Number words for the numbers 1-20 in the dialect spoken around the Buenaventura Mission are given in Table 2. An examination of this list reveals how the root words for the first four numerals are combined and modified to form other numerals and that the names of the other numerals relate to *four* or a multiple or power of *four*. Beeler states that the reason the Chumash used a system based on *four* has been lost, but that speakers of languages with similar counting systems report holding sticks or bundles between the fingers when counting them (four spaces between fingers on a hand). Such a system makes sense for a hunter-gatherer society such as the Chumash.

Table 2 shows that the additive logic underlying the Chumash number system was not unlike that underlying our own. For example, 12 is *maseg scumu*, or three times four; 13 is *masegscumu canpaqueet*, or three times four plus one. The oral number system then becomes subtractive, not unlike the written one of the Romans.

Table 2
Chumash Number Words, Ventureno Dialect

1	paqueet	11	telu
2	eshcom	12	maseg scumu
3	maseg	13	masegscumu canpaqueet
4	scumu	14	eshcom laliet
5	itipaques	15	paqueet cihue
6	yetishcom	16	chigipsh
7	itimaseg	17	chigipsh canpaqueet
8	malahua	18	eshcom cihue scumuhuy
9	etspa	19	paqueet cihue scumuhuy
10	cashcom	20	scumuhuy

Source: Adapted from Beeler, 1990.

Fourteen is *eshcom laliet*, or "two lacking" (from sixteen), while 15 is *paqueet cihue*, or "one lacking" (from sixteen). In a base four system, the number representing four fours is very important, and is given its own name, *chigipsh*, a term associated with completeness or lacking nothing. In our system, ten tens represents a completes set of hands of hands, and is given the special name *hundred*, while in Oscar's world, eight eights would represent this complete set (although we don't know what he would call it). While the written symbols used in the number systems may vary from ours to Oscar's to the Chumash, the principles on which the systems are based are not too different.

The gap from the Chumash base four system to the western base ten system was bridged when the Chumash were visited by Spanish explorers in the late 1700's. Jose Senan (1760-1823), stationed at Mission San Buenaventura from 1797 until the end of his life, recounts the following conversation between himself and the Chumash as recorded in Senan's personal diary.

"Question: To how many have you said that what the Father says is a lie?

Answer: To fourteen (eshcom laliet). This expression in Ventureno means something like 'two lacking, subtract two.'

Question: I don't understand what you say to me. I don't understand the way you people count: count by tens.

Answer: Ten and four (*cashcom casatscumu*)" #(Beeler, 1990, p. 111).

While Senan clearly did not understand the Chumash number system, the Chumash speaker understood Senan's base ten system, and was able to express the number in a way that Senan would understand. Although the context of the conversation is not given, Senan seems to be accusing the Chumash of doubting the Father's words, an ironic twist in a conversation in which it was the Chumash speaker who needed to explain things in a form that the visitor could understand.

Inuit Number System

Although also a hunter-gatherer society, the Inuit of northern Canada developed a very different counting system, with the significant numerals being *five, ten* and *twenty.* A sampling of numbers in the Inuit system is given in Table 3. In examining these numbers, J. Peter Denny (1990) notes that there are independent terms for *one* through *five* and special terms for *five, ten,* and *twenty.* Other number words are formed by adding words which indicate orientation in relation to body parts.

Table 3
Inuit Number Words

1	atasusiq	12	itikkanuuqtuut maqruungnik
2	maqruuk	13	itikkanuuqtuut pingasunik
3	pingasut	14	itikkanuuqtuut sitamanik
4	sitamat	15	itikkanuuqtuut tallimanik
5	tallimat (refers to arm)	16	arviqtangat (refers to the right foot)
6	arvinilik atausirmik (refers to the right hand)	17	arvitanganit aqraqtut
7	arvinilik maqruungnik	18	arvitanganit pingasut
8	arvinilik pingasunik	19	arvitanganit sitam at
9	arvinilik sitamanik	20	avatit (related to limbs, or completion of counting on all four limbs
10	qulit (refers to 'top,' meaning the hands)	100	avatit tallimat (twenty's five)
11	itikkanuuqtuut atausirmik (refers to the feet)		

Source: Adapted from Denny, 1990.

Denny suggests that the Inuit system is determined by counting on fingers and toes, a system which reflects an organization of thought which is typical in hunting societies. By basing a system so closely on counting fingers and toes, with a prescribed sequence of the limb used, strong connections across domains are present so that "one set of ideas is always seen in the context of another set. In this case, the sequence of numbers is supported by the context of anatomical structure." Denny, in reviewing Gerald Noelting's work (Baillargeon, et. al., 1977), indicates that Noelting "suggests that counting proceeds from left to right because of further linkage of left-right to east-west and thereby to the rising and setting of the sun—left is thus a beginning and right an end point" (p. 139).

Other Number Systems

Marcia Ascher, in her book *Ethnomathematics: A Multicultural View of Mathematical Ideas* (1991), also addresses the role of context in number systems when she describes the system of the inhabitants of the Gilbert Islands of Micronesia. These islanders support themselves by fishing and eating fruit and other plants which grow wild on the islands. Their number system contains linguistic classifiers which become affixed to the number words and which indicate the characteristics of the item being counted. For instance, the word *six* differs slightly based on whether the items being counted are, for example, groups of humans, bundles of thatch, or baskets.[5] This degree of specificity of the language of the counting system is not surprising in a society which is dependent on its immediate environment for survival.

In contrast to the Chumash, Inuit, and Gilbert Islanders, some societies have little use for counting systems which handle individual items but have much use for the development of observational abilities which allow them to determine if all are present in a large group. Claudia Zaslavsky (1973) relates the story of an African nomadic sheepherder who had difficulty understanding the process of bartering four sticks of tobacco for two sheep, but was immediately able to tell when one sheep was missing from a large flock.[6] His ability to keep track of the herd was dependent on his keen observational abilities which enabled him to know each sheep individually, rather than his ability to count them according to common attributes using an elaborate number system (p. 32). In fact, counting human beings, animals, or valuable possessions was taboo for spiritual reasons in some societies, thereby encouraging the development of observational abilities over the language of counting.

Arithmetic Operations

J. Peter Denny (1990) suggests that arithmetic operations (addition, subtraction, multiplication, and division) are needed to manipulate the numerical values of objects rather than the objects themselves, and that the need for these operations arises out of the economic structure of a society. He states that, "the main condition under which arithmetical operations become useful is economic action at a distance.... The basic role of the arithmetic operations is to permit manipulation of the numerical values of objects as a substitute for the manipulation of the objects themselves" (p. 156). This kind of mathematics is needed in a society in which workers are specialized, such as in an agricultural or industrialized society in which the one doing the trading is not the one involved in growing or making the product. The language of the mathematics in agricultural/ industrial societies mirrors this value in that it is very economical. Key variables are isolated and controlled, and context is kept out of the equation as much as possible. Consider the expression 2 + 3, which can be easily stated and simplified to 5. The same relationship would be expressed in the Inuit culture as *marruuglu pingasudlu katillagik tadlimaguqtut*, which means "two and three and someone joining them they become five" (the suffix lu essentially means "and"or "too"). Within the linguistic expression of this equation is a concrete description of the arithmetic process needed to solve the problem, along with an awareness of the individual completing the process. If the numbers included in this equation are compared to the list presented in Table 2 we see that they are somewhat different. The difference reflects changes made to the number words based on the context in which the applications occur.

The arithmetic operation of division provides particularly interesting clues into how mathematical thought develops as a result of experience. In spite of the typical sharing of necessities in a hunter/gatherer society, the arithmetic operation of division appeared absent until trading with other cultures began. J. Peter Denny suggests that

> ...numerical value becomes important only when dealing with unknown or indistinguishable elements. Traditional methods of dividing game preserve the distinct anatomical identity of each share. Inuit, when sharing a seal, divide it into specified anatomical parts which are the proper share of particular relatives of the hunter. The seal is never treated as a homogenous mass of seal meat whose bulk would have to be assessed numerically and then divided into parts whose size was determined by arithmetical division (1990, p. 158).

In expressing numerical division, Inuit forms are vague and difficult to express, with the same form taking different meanings according to context. This is consistent with the increased emphasis in this culture on the environment and relationships within the group, along with the lack of emphasis placed on numerical value in general.

Geometry

Geometry results from one's attempt to organize space. Industrialized societies have long depended on Euclidean geometry (and, more recently, non-Euclidean geometry) to describe the physical world. Straight lines and clean angles have been associated with an ordered and controlled environment. With increased industrialization, the exactness of these lines and angles becomes crucial, as parts of objects become inter-changeable and commercial items must be identical to those advertised. Euclid himself developed vocabulary to describe the relationships between triangles, angles, segments, and lines. The emphasis was on dividing a whole into parts, with regular figures (such as an equilateral triangle, square, etc.) being more highly valued than irregular ones.

The Romanesque architecture of Notre Dame cathedral and the Gothic architecture of Chartes cathedral are tributes to the architects' mathematical ability and understanding of geometry. In both French cathedrals the exactness of the lines and angles used were fundamental to creating structures which were physically sound, yet would draw the worshippers' attention upward towards heaven. The sweeping angles themselves, particularly in the cathedral of Chartes, communicated the architect's view of God.

In hunter/gatherer societies there is sensitivity to the irregularities of shapes and particular emphasis on describing curves found in the natural world. For example, the Navajo of the southwestern United States see their environment as dynamic and continuously changing. Where Western thought takes a moment in time and freezes it to study more closely, the Navajo sees motion as intrinsic to all things. Even spatial boundaries such as mountains are in motion and in the process of being changed. Thus, spatial concepts, when described in the Navajo language, are expressed using numerous conjunctions (more than 300,000) of the verb translated as "to go," with verb forms of "to be" rarely used. When objects overlap, the overlap is because of a process of change. For instance, the overlap that occurs when a snake is on a rock must be defined in terms of whether the snake is sleeping on the rock or slithering over it. In Western thought, it is typical to think of overlap as static, with the region in common being the significant point (Ascher, 1991, pp. 129-130).

Where industrialized societies rely heavily on angles, lines, and planes, hunter/gatherer societies such as the Sioux hold great appreciation for curves and round shapes because of the connection to the sun, the earth, the stars, the seasons, and the life cycle. Teepees are round and always placed in a circle[7] (Ascher, 1991, p. 125). The languages of hunter/gatherer societies are rich in description of natural shapes. For example, consider these examples describing the curvature of a rope from the language of the Ojibway of Canada (Denny, 1990):

Noonima (curve in the body of the rope)
Waawiyeyaa (curve at the end of the rope)
Waagaa (curvature of the axis of the rope)

Thus, while industrialized societies look at geometry as a tool for building and finding patterns, hunter/gatherers look at geometry as a means of appreciating what occurs in nature. The Inuit saw nature as fundamentally ambiguous, and this perception was reflected in their art. A carving, for example, can often be interpreted in more than one way, a "seasonal pun." In the words of Heather Smith Siska, author of the beautiful children's book *People of the Ice*,

Sometimes, especially during the long winter months, the Inuit carved shapes of animals or people purely for pleasure. But a carver did not just pick up a stone and begin to work on it. He held it, thought about it and felt it all over. The Inuit believed there was an image within each stone that would be freed when it was carved, that its soul would be released. In this, as in all other aspects of Inuit life, there was harmony between man and nature (Siska, 1995, p. 43).

Measurement

As with number systems, arithmetic operations, and geometry, measurement in non-industrialized societies relies on highly developed perceptual skills. Distance may be measured in number of sleeps and time measured in pipe smokes (*ningodopwaagan* in the language of the Ojibway). As with all mathematical thought in hunter/gatherer societies, the language related to measurement is context sensitive to give the maximum amount of information (Denny, 1990).

It is typically the case in hunter/gatherer societies that the designer and builder of an object are the same person, thereby eliminating the need for objective precision in units of measurement. Whereas industrialized societies use objective terms such as millimeters, centimeters, and meters, hunter/gatherer societies use subjective terms such as the length of a body part. The U.S. system using inches, feet, and yards was originally based on parts of the human body with an inch corresponding to the distance to the first knuckle of the thumb, four palms equal to a foot, and one pace in walking equal to a yard. This system was standardized because of increased trade and specialization of workers within the society. For instance, a door made in Florence needed to fit a cathedral in Milan (Zaslavsky, 1973). Hunter/gatherer societies retained the use of body parts for measurement out of necessity. For one who moves frequently, it is necessary to keep equipment at a minimum. Use of body parts ensured standardization for one's own work and was easy to remember[8] (Denny, 1990).

Summary

The experience of Oscar the Grouch and the Cerean waitress provides a way to compare our familiar base ten system with the counting system of other possible worlds. Indeed, the mathematics of the Chumash and Inuit illustrate how non-base ten number systems, geometric shapes, and units of measurement are constructed as a means of describing collective and individual experience. The mathematical richness of these cultures is evident in the way that objects are described or even defined by the mathematical language used to communicate their properties. By comparison, our mathematical system teaches and rewards the ability to abstract number from the object being named.[9] In developing an awareness of cultures different from our own, we may be able to more fully realize that mathematics is not a static subject but a dynamic process in which mathematical language and symbols describe and influence the experience and values of the society.

Footnotes

1. We would like to express our appreciation to Dr. Philip Dreyer for inviting us to be part of the 1995 Claremont Reading Conference, and to Dr. Rick Luttmann for his many helpful edits and suggestions for the manuscript.

2. Matt Groening's cartoon characters Bart and Lisa Simpson had a wry exchange in an episode of Fox-TV's *The Simpsons*. Of course, like most cartoon characters, each of their hands has four digits. In the episode, Lisa, reading from a book, announces to Bart that "scientists have predicted that people in the distant future will evolve to have *four* fingers and a thumb on each hand." Bart replies, "Oooh, gross!"

3. Some number words, such as those for 11 and 12, do not follow the number pattern, but have their own names, usually rooted in history. For example, the old Anglo-Saxon word "endleofan" meant "and one left." Since people counted on their fingers then "endleofan" wound up as our word "eleven." (Boyd, 1994, p. C1).

4. One such example is that of the Yurok Indians who, though they have five fingers just as we do, count on the *four* spaces between their fingers, and hence like Oscar have a base eight number system.

5. This word variation property is true of the Ojibway as well. They have different suffixes for number words to denote geometric properties of the objects being counted.

6. Similarly, in South America, a hunter cannot name the number of arrows in his quiver but can tell immediately if one is missing.

7. As are igloos, hogans, yurts, and mengattos—always round.

8. This is significant. For example, you build a canoe for yourself so of course *your* body parts should be used to measure. Thus, the canoe will fit *you.*

9. Indeed, algebra is perhaps the ultimate expression of this, for both the object and the number of those objects become irrelevant.

References

Allen, C. (1990). *Oscar's grouchy sounds.* Sesame
    Street/Golden Press, Western Publishing Company.

Ascher, M. (1991). *Ethnomathematics: A multicultural view of mathematical ideas.* Pacific Grove, CA: Brooks-Cole.

Baillargeon, R., Noelting, G., Dorais, L-J., and Saladin d'Anglure, B. (1977). "Aspects semantiques et structuraux de la numeration chez les Inuit." *Etudes Inuit,* 1, pp. 93-128.

Beeler, M. S. (1990). "Chumash numerals." In M. P. Closs (Ed.) *Native American mathematics.* Austin, TX: University of Texas Press, pp. 109-128.

Boyd, L. M. (1994). "The grab bag." *San Francisco Chronicle.* October 15, p. C1.

Children's Television Network. (CTW, 1991). *One rubber duckie: A Sesame street counting book.*

Closs, M. P. (ed). (1986). *Native American mathematics.* Austin, TX: University of Texas Press.

Denny, J. P. (1990). "Cultural ecology of mathematics: Ojibway and Inuit hunters." In M. P. Closs (Ed.), *Native American mathematics.* Austin, TX: University of Texas Press, pp. 129-180.

Ellis, J. (1993). *Language, thought, and logic.* Evanston, IL: Northwestern University Press.

Siska, H. S. (1995). *People of the ice: How the Inuit live.* Buffalo, NY: Firefly Books.

Zaslavsky, C. (1973). *Africa counts: Number and pattern in African culture.* NY: Lawrence Hill.

ON HATING POETRY

OR

HOW I CAME TO WRITE
Good Luck Gold and Other Poems

Janet S. Wong

As a child, I hated poetry. I hated it because I found it difficult to read out loud, with all the decisions about where to pause. I hated it because I couldn't identify with most of what I read. I especially hated those dense poems by dead English poets. I still do.

Four years ago, when I left the practice of law to do something good with my life, I decided to start by writing the next *Charlotte's Web.* In between this serious novel writing, I thought I might try to write a picture book, too—maybe one a week! But then—as if I were being punished for such arrogance—I found myself stuck in a room one morning, listening to Myra Cohn Livingston talk about poetry.

It was at a Saturday UCLA Extension seminar on how to write and sell a children's book. I had come for the part about selling, and wanted to hear the editor speak on how to market a manuscript. I groaned when I learned that I was going to have to sit through twenty minutes of poetry before the part on marketing. I shifted in my seat, doodled, stared out the window. Then Myra read the title poem from ..er book *There Was a Place and Other Poems* (McElderry Books) and the next thing I knew I was blinking back tears. I am not the kind that cries in public.

Three months later—even though I still hated poetry—I signed up for Myra's class.

I entered her class with no intention of writing poetry for publication. I thought I would like to learn to write rhythmic prose, to writing something like *Goodnight Moon*. I had never heard the words couplet or tercet or quatrain before, and three weeks into her class I proudly guessed that a cinquain was a poem with five lines that rhymed. If pressed to answer, I might have defined pentameter as an Olympic event.

Still, I was determined to learn about meter and rhyme, and each week grew increasingly disappointed by the absence of happy faces or any other sign of praise on my homework. In fact, there were so few marks on my homework each week that I began to wonder if she actually read it at all. Eleven weeks after I had begun to study with Myra Cohn Livingston, I finally received the first substantive comment on a piece of homework. It looked like a comment, at least: *u.q.* After puzzling for two hours on what "u.q." could possibly mean, I mustered the courage to ask Myra. "That's 'v.g.,' dear," she said, looking at me as if I were impossible, hopeless. "*Very good.*" That poem, "Waiting at the Railroad Cafe," is my favorite poem in *Good Luck Gold and Other Poems* (McElderry/Simon & Schuster), for the simple reason that it is the first poem of mine Myra ever liked.

Waiting at the Railroad Cafe

All the white kids are eating.
"Let's go, Dad," I say.
"Let's go out of this place."
But Dad doesn't move.
He's going to prove

the Asian race
is equal. We stay
and take our silent beating.

He folds his arms
across his chest
glaring at the waitresses who
pass by like cattle
ready for a western battle.
They will not look, they refuse to
surrender even to my best
wishing on bracelet charms.

"Consider this part of your education,"
Dad says. I wonder how long
we'll be ignored, like hungry ghosts
of Chinese men who laid this track,
never making their journeys back
but leaving milestones and signposts
to follow. "Why do they treat us so wrong?"
I wonder. "Don't they know we're on vacation?"

A drunk shouts at us and
gets louder and redder
in the face
when we pay
him no mind. I say
"Let's get out of this place.
We're not equal. We're better,"
as I pull Dad by the hand.

I think Myra liked this poem because it was one of the first
serious poems I had written—my first poem on racism, and the
first poem I had written with some meaning beyond myself.

Before that, most of my work fell into the category of light verse, poems on pimples and dog poop, stuff I thought kids would like. Very little of what I wrote was "ethnic" because, as much as I wanted to sell my work, I bristled at the idea of profiting from my ethnicity. I did not understand that since many of my significant memories involve my family, many of my best stories will be Asian American too.

"Waiting at the Railroad Cafe" is based on an incident that happened to me the summer between eighth and ninth grade, while I was traveling with my father to Yellowstone. With Myra's encouragement, I began to write more poems about issues of race. Here is the poem "Noise:"

Noise

Ching chong Chinaman

>Those kids over there
>are laughing at me.
>My hair.
>My nose
>My skin.

>I hear the noise.
Ching chong
>>I won't let it in.

>They're pulling their lids
>up, down and out
>to the side,
>making wide eyes slit thin,
>faking being
>some kind of Chinese

I've never seen,
chanting
ching chong ching chong
Open your eyes
Open your eyes, Chinese

It's only noise.
ching chong
I won't let it in.
I won't let it in.

I promise myself

I won't let them
win.

The impetus for "Noise" was a conversation I had with my
mother three years go. I had just participated in a teach-in on
multiculturalism where I heard a preschool teacher complain that
the classmates of a Korean child were taunting him with "Ching
Chong Chinaman" while pulling at their eyes. Later, when I had
dinner with my parents, I told them I was surprised that children
this young could be so mean. My mother said: "They used to do
this to you all the time. You would come home crying. Don't
you remember?" I didn't. I guess I had refused, as a kind of
self-defense, to "let it in." The only incident I remember
happened when I was a student at Yale Law School. Walking to
the market one day, I suddenly found myself being pursued by a
group of boys on bikes, chanting "Ching Chong, Ching Chong"
and laughing. As I wrote "Noise," I remembered the weather
that day, and the look of the New Haven neighborhood I had
walked through with them following me a full block. But I
could not remember the face of even one boy.

Almost all of the poems in *Good Luck Gold* are based on personal experience, the experience of a friend, or observation. But because not all of my experiences are "Asian-themed," not all of my poems are "Asian-themed" either. Sometimes this seems to cause difficulties. In my second book, *A Suitcase of Seaweed*, which is divided into Korean, Chinese and American sections, there is a poem called "Our Daily Bread." I have placed this poem in the American section of the book, although many children of Asian immigrants, whose sometimes college-educated families often run restaurants and mini-marts, will identify with it.

Our Daily Bread

Nine p.m. we close the store,
wash the counter, mop the floor.

Ten p.m. we finally eat.
Father pulls a milk crate seat

to the table and we pray
Thank you for this crazy day.

Before the book was divided into sections, I asked a writer friend whom I respect and like a great deal to read the manuscript. When I read her comments on this poem, I was saddened. "Could you make this poem seem more authentic?" she wrote. "Perhaps the milk crate could be something else." Something else! What? A soy sauce can? Visiting my parents' market in Oregon last week, I noticed that they use their empty soy sauce containers to store golf balls.

I still have not written the next *Charlotte's Web*, or the next *Goodnight Moon*. Nearly all I write is poetry, perhaps because nearly all I read is poetry, and mainly poetry for children. I cherish the thoughtful poems that Myra Cohn Livingston and Deborah Chandra write, the clever poems crafted by Alice Schertle and J. Patrick Lewis, the quirky images of Cynthia Ryland and Gary Soto, Monica Gunning's rich pictures of her Jamaican home. I read the Asian American poets Marilyn Chin, Lawson Fusao Inada, Garrett Hongo and Mitsuye Yamada, always looking—as you probably are, too—for something fresh to share with children, something to make them stretch. The greatest compliment I receive from children—and there seems to be one child at every school who tells me this—is "I used to hate poetry, but after hearing you, I like it." I hope one of you longtime poetry-haters out there feels that way now, too.

"Waiting at the Railroad Cafe" and "Noise" from *Good Luck Gold* and "Our Daily Bread" from the forthcoming book *A Suitcase of Seaweed* (Spring 1996) are used by permission from Margaret K. McElderry Books, an imprint of the Simon & Schuster Children's Publishing Division.

TO LEARN THREE THOUSAND "LETTERS:" EARLY LITERACY IN CHINA

John Regan
Hao Ke-Qi
Huang Ping-An
Zhang Wei-Jiang
Yang Chang-Qing

Is there any value in exploring the ways another culture goes about teaching children to read? We are now convinced there is. The following explains why:

On the front page of a Chinese newspaper published in Beijing, an article appeared about teaching reading in New Zealand. The article mentioned a "reading war" between advocates of a "whole word" and a "phonics" approach to the teaching of children's reading. Elsewhere in the news report was mentioned the types of reading problems of children who had been taught by one or the other of those methods.

Several Chinese educators, who were sitting by during a discussion of this article among some American visitors, became interested. They said that they did not understand this issue mentioned in the paper which we were discussing, especially the point about "reading problems." What were "reading problems"?

"What do you mean by reading problems?" said one of the Chinese. The American educators looked momentarily puzzled and then one of them, somewhat in jest, replied,

What do you mean by 'what do you mean'? You know....
'problems.' Children have problems in learning to read, and
we are always looking for solutions. This matter even can
become a political issue as is also the case in the United
States.

But it is not a problem, is it?" responded one Chinese
professor of English. "Perhaps it is just a lot of hard work to
learn to read, and I think by Grade 6 everyone can read, but
only after careful, disciplined repetitions and hard work.
There are no problems, really. I don't understand why you
say there are reading problems.

A conversation was clearly developing and one of the
Americans leaned forward and said,

Now it is I who do not understand! I don't know what you
mean. With your writing system, your schools must have
horrendous problems. To be literate your children need to
learn 5,000 characters. With us, everyone knows about
children having difficulty unlocking the reading code of
learning to read. It is one of the schools' main problems.
Must be the same, surely, with you.

Soon these educators from opposite sides of the Pacific
were thoroughly involved in a broader topic of differences
between their two cultures' reading and writing programs. As
this continued, it became clear from the expressions and
reactions of each side that some considerable gaps separated
their understanding of some quite basic issues about learning to
read. What seemed to the Westerners to be simple statements
about basic educational realities, the Chinese did not understand
or had quite contrary views.

Both sets of educators' incredulous looks seemed to increase as each new topic was brought up. For example, at one point an American said, "Despite all the problems our children have in schools learning to read, many children, of course, just learn to read on their own."

The puzzled faces of the four Chinese caused the speaker to frown, pause, then to make this following expansion on his statement.

> You know! Some children just pick up how to read by noticing words around them, on television, etc. They more or less get the fact that reading is learning a code, and they break the code. Or they just learn a lot of the words as whole pieces and then learn the code—what the letters stand for and go on from there.

Madam Hao, one of the distinguished Chinese educators, broke in, "That's not possible, surely. How could a child learn to read on her own? It's quite impossible in my opinion."

The other Chinese educator nodded in agreement as the teachers' college dean added,

> What I say is, what you say is impossible. There is no way I can imagine that. If my daughter learned 10 characters, 20, 50, 100, this does not help her learn the next 50—or (at least only in a very, very general way). It's not like morse code, you know. Writing, at least in China, is not like a situation where you learn a couple of dozen parts, and you can unlock everything else. Anyway, there is no way that a child can learn to read on his own.

The discussion would come back to this point and also the earlier disagreement. But at this point we want to explain the next step in the process by which we began to understand each other's positions across our cultural divide.

The Americans were confused at what was going on. Were the Chinese being too polite or proud to acknowledge the nature of, for example, children's reading problems? At first we thought this seemed a reasonable possibility. But then, no matter from what angle we approached the topic, we could not get beyond our Asian colleagues' firm and widely accepted conviction that success in reading was a natural result only of effort. Learning to read required simply hard work, practice, hundreds of hours of it. The school's timetable ensured this. There was no chance a child could learn on his or her own. Even illiteracy was considered the result of lack of concerted effort. What (the Chinese told us later they had thought) could be behind these American's opinion about such obvious facts?

We wanted to know more about this puzzling situation separating our discussion of literacy.

- To be literate a Chinese child would by Grade 6 be able to recognize about 5,000 different shape clusters (out of the 40,000-50,000 character system). Fine, we understood that.
- English words were all constructed with 26 shapes (and capital forms). Yes, agreed.
- These Chinese characters and clusters of characters that made up the reading page were each in some form visually different. Again, understood.
- These "geometric" architectural differences altered the meaning.
- These shapes didn't "spell" the word, they just displayed it.

- While words in English also are all different in shape, they all use the same 26 letters.

We began pulling all this and more together and began asking questions:

So what if children come across a character that they do not recognize? The Chinese child's options for discovering its meaning (without asking someone or looking it up in a dictionary) were not the same as the English-speaking child has in using the alphabetic code. One option not available for the Chinese child was sounding out that word to see if perhaps he/she might have heard the word before. Possible for a Western child. Not possible for a Chinese.

We began a program of observations and interviews in schools and homes. All roads led to the same conclusions: Intense school and homework repetition was the solution for any problem of learning to read in China. And the Western educators had to agree there did seem to be a high success rate.

As facts and attitudes began to fall into place, the Westerners became increasingly impressed with the enormous task of Chinese children's learning to read, but were still puzzled by a torrent of issues.

"How is it possible to know a meaning and not be able to say it?"
"Why do the children have to learn the *names* of all the strokes and in sequence in the writing of a character?"
"What sort of homework is given?"
"How is a reading teacher trained?" etc.

To get at such questions, and a host of others too numerous to mention, a questionnaire was constructed. Meanwhile, in the following somewhat humorous way, we discovered how dramatically different were the two reading/writing "semiotic" (orthography) systems.

I can't call him "pig" or "spider," can I?

If you ask a Chinese to write someone's Western name in character form, typically you will notice hesitation and delay. Sometimes the fumble goes on for such a long time that a Westerner may become irritated. It seems that doing this for a friend should be such a simple task to—write a name in the other writing system. So what's the delay?

We witnessed exactly this sort of irritation when one of our associates asked a Chinese woman student he knew to write his nickname "Drew" (for Andrew) in character form. The young visitor hesitated and, after some pause, said that she would bring it next time that they met.

Andrew was somewhat annoyed. This "next time" was to be the following week. And he had begun to like her before this.

"What in the world is she so perplexed about?" he was heard to say. "Can't she just write my name? Surely, I haven't asked anything difficult?"

But, in fact, Drew had asked a question which presented a real problem for Miss Chang. In the reason for this fact lies a tale of interest to reading educators (it was to the Western visitors) and helped put things in focus.

Of the three Chinese characters for "Drew" that Miss Chang first pulled up in her visual memory, one stood for "pig," another for "kill," another for "cattle pole." Each of these was a different character but *not* a different sound. What characters and, hence, what meaning would Miss Chang select? Not one of these! She needed her dictionary and some time to think. There were some score or more of different characters, each of which had different (sometimes obnoxious meanings). But all of these, when spoken, *sounded like* "Drew." It turned out that this was the very same fact with thousands of characters—same sound but many, many meanings, and hence characters. Each character was a different meaning, sometimes only because of one small dot or line or twist in the architecture of the complex shape.

None of the meanings for these first characters seemed to be appropriate—"spider," "dwarf," "water on the ground" (and again "cattle pole," "kill," "pig") and so on. Hence, Miss Chang certainly needed to go further in her search if she were not to assign a ridiculous character to Andrew's nickname. She decided that two of these characters—one meaning "beads," and the other "a kind of grass"—were at least reasonable. But there was another step yet to consider and, therefore, she needed to look at her two choices to see which one she thought had a nicer shape. Pleasantness of shape was in itself a factor that she felt obliged to consider in her choice—quite apart from her own calligraphy.

We could now see clearly as we learned about this matter that the original delay was the result of Miss Chang's earnest searching for just the right character. What a misunderstanding! To be correct and appropriate, the choice she would give as her decision would need to

–sound like Drew,
–have a meaning that was respectful,
–be a shape she liked,
–be good handwriting.

The Chinese have a different theory of orthography. The Chinese appeared astonished that we did not know all this, for them, obvious reality.

We discovered that for the child learning words, rarely do the characters guide the tongue to sound, but only the eye to meaning. Perhaps, the Westerners speculated, that situation is similar to that which someone would experience if she were living in another country and could recognized the visual signs on a street (that stood for "open," or "closed," or "men," or "women,") but did not know how to *say* those words in that language.

One of our interests in the strategies young Chinese learners used for getting meaning from characters was the topic of "subvocalization." Another was "dyslexia." This interest began by working with an amazing young Western woman who told a reading clinician that she had found a way to halt her perceptual problem of letters seeming to move on a page. She placed her fingers over the next shapes in the line of print until she needed to see them and would then uncover them. This type and solution to her reading problem of "moving shapes" caused us to speculate on how the strategy of this young woman could possibly work in the Chinese writing system. When we considered the basic literacy 5,000 shapes (with such a plethora of "moveable" parts), we were convinced that there would be hundreds of times more similar difficulties in China. But we did not find that to be so at all. More puzzlement. Because of our developing interest in the topic, we decided to hold a conference on this whole topic.

At this symposium, to give those attending a sense of the Chinese learners' task (not to mention the reading teachers' necessary effort), we began the day's session by writing a sentence in Chinese on the board.

Under that we wrote an English translation. The audience of over 60 people was asked to study these Chinese characters, to look very carefully at the shapes—each dense with lines, angles—and to try to learn them well enough to be able to recognize them in pages of other characters. Clearly, in terms of lines, all of these were not only unfamiliar but also more complex in form than any English word's letter. On the other hand, these characters were almost all a whole meaning, or meanings, not alphabet-type parts of a word. After ten minutes of the audience's trying, we discussed the results. We would have all failed a Grade 1 test in China.

Just to distinguish and then recognize those characters was a visual memory task that would take great focused looking and visual acuity, practice upon practice. The Chinese homework sheets and workbooks showed that to be so. And what about the learning of the motor skills for reproducing the characters? If after an arduous program of self study, members of our conference had learned to recognize each of these shapes, they would know the meanings but not know how to say them. For the audience to learn enough to equal what the first grade Chinese reader/writer could do, they would need to know as well

—that the lines and angles had to be written in a strict sequence
—that each of these shapes had a name

–that these names for each step—sometimes over twenty steps—had to be learned also.

Next we revised our questionnaire to examine attitudes and viewpoints of Chinese and Western parents and educators. Had anyone present heard of, or had personal acquaintance with, reading problems? The Westerners, as predicted on the basis of the above, responded overwhelmingly in the affirmative. The variety of suggestions for solutions was extensive and varied. Had the Westerners heard of children who had learned to read on their own? Yes they had. But the majority thought a bright, aware child could learn on his own. Would it be possible to learn to read by being a sharp observer? Of course, they knew children who had learned to read on their own. What were adults' views of the time required for success in reading? What was the amount of effort needed by a Grade 6 to read a newspaper? So went the questions.

For the Chinese again, learning to read was seen to be a very difficult task, requiring energetic adherence to a strict learning plan, an unwavering program of massive practices. Was learning to read a skill which a child could achieve on his own without a teacher? "No," replied the Chinese.

The dramatic difference in the two cultures' responses could not be easily explained away. A significantly different curriculum and teaching method must be in existence for such an actual learning task.

Learning About Ourselves

Books explicating reasons for the American children's sometimes low levels of reading ability have been best sellers over generations. Parental, political groups and movements supporting alternative approaches have occupied enormous space in the literature. Philosophies and alternative approaches have been advertised. Despite this complexity of efforts, learning to read is seen in the West by significant numbers of adults as not so difficult that many children could not master it on their own. Our encounter with contradictory views had brought to our own awareness much of what we assumed about reading.

It is difficult to look objectively at our own cultural assumptions. Indeed, often the more we know of a topic, for example in this case reading, the more difficult it is to take an outside view—to see alternatives. In the above discussion, the individuals from one culture often had a very hard time understanding what the other group was talking about, despite the fact that the topic was such a significant and basic part of schooling. Ironically, the Chinese initially were themselves convinced that the Westerner's reports could not possibly be true. How could a task of learning 26 shapes be a problem? And so the incredulous questions continued.

Learning about ourselves from studying another culture involves resisting the temptation to make judgments as to which one of those customs is better. Each unique society socializes to its own special relevance. Questions of "better" cannot be logically asked. A teaching strategy, or method, etc., is forever part of the whole fabric of the culture and can rarely be picked out, transferred, and used in another. Therefore, what we learn from comparisons of ourselves with others need to be considered as examples of what is done in the world (and done perhaps successfully), but not entirely translatable. Still there are lessons of sorts to be learned.

Influences Spreading From
One Cultural Habit to Another

We concluded that the Chinese group which began to talk to the Americans about that New Zealand "reading war" article was, in large measure, quite right in what they had said. We discovered much on the way to our own understanding; for example, we learned that very young children, at surprisingly early ages, in both cultures, catch the general outline of their writing system as a result of their seeing writing in their environment. We discovered that other related learning seeps into the young learners' consciousness from their own culture's writing and reading process; that, for example, who "pretend" to write, do box-like character shapes quite unlike the products of their American brothers and sisters. And another example, many Chinese apply the "straight line" principle of a Chinese page to writing in English letters. Being accustomed to the equally shaped boxes of a character and the consequent evenness of a page left and right—the straight edge of writing on both left and right hand side of a page— printers who do not know English writing will break up words in creative ways—on one line a non-English speaker might copy (for the word "American") "A" at the end of one line, or "Am," or "Ame," and finish it on the next, replicating the precision orderliness of the Chinese writer's page.

We were surprised to discover how perfectly Grade 1 Chinese children could reproduce a character which they had never seen before (and after looking for 10 brief seconds). Their eyes and hands were attuned to these shapes even at Grade 1. With five years more of intense daily training before them, how much more would their behavior show the influence of their reading?

When we asked Western youngsters of similar age to do the same task, their reproductions were not in a line—not in any way equal in size and the results looked as embarrassingly strange as our own efforts.

We have learned something larger than all this—something about what we as human beings can do. We have found out more about the capacities and flexibilities of one of our human, meaning-making channels—the ability to associate visual form and meaning. In this theme, we conclude with a section from one of our author's other publications.

The human mind is a wondrous thing, and we should be continually amazed by its capacity to pursue one way of representing the world, even unto the most complex of results. There is, for example, the Chinese writing system and its success....

...No one told the Chinese to stop their excellent history of representing what they wanted to say and think in shapes that directly meant. Had they stopped, we would never have discovered how infinitely marvelous this one facet of the visual side of our meaning-making, our semiotic potential, might be. As it is, we now have a chance to know what human beings may become, given the tenacious insistence on cultivating one form of representation and all the richness of cultural phenomena to which it gives rise.

...For thousands of years the Chinese have furthered this effort of basically direct semantic references rather than passing meaning through shapes which stand for sound. The result is a vast, visually based, logical writing system. Based on my observational studies as well as more formal investigations in China, I have slowly come to suspect that this massive ideographic-iconographic-logographic—or whatever one calls it—system of writing which is learned by a Chinese from early ages is a part of, coordinates with, sets in motion other habits, skills, customs, and interests. It is, if not the centerpiece, then the most obvious part in a network of interrelating behaviors, customs, practices, attitudes, and artifacts which a visitor experiences every day in China....

...Is the Chinese interest in the appearance and the importance of words different from ours? Is the dragon's eye a different one from the Westerners'? Does the Chinese child practice early a unique accuracy in seeing, recording, recalling, and contemplating two-dimensional character kinds of phenomena?

...The Western alphabetic shapes on this page are drawn from the 26 relatively simple forms (with the addition of some capital forms, commas, etc.). With some additional combinations, like "th," "ch," "sh," we arrive at the logic of our writing system! The shapes stand for sound, the Chinese shapes do not. When we write "tree" or "mountain" or "forest," we make these shapes out of our 26 letters. For the Chinese, there are about 40,000 characters and only 4,000 syllables. Hence, there is more for the mind to remember visually than there is for the ear to deal with acoustically.

...Imagine that everything which we named in the world was named in a way that we thought looked like its meaning. Imagine that we became habituated to recalling such meaning by writing, tracing on the hand or in the air, thinking shapes. More importantly, imagine that we had to distinguish between linguistic meaning ... only in our mind's eye, for we could not say the distinction—that there were an approximate ten-to-one ratio of shapes to sound—ten ways to write something that can be said.[1]

Footnote

1. John Regan, "Eye of the Dragon," the Thirteenth Symposium in the series, *Issues in Communication*, Claremont University Press, 1988.

A page of homework practice (marked by teacher) found in a small ancient village in Shaanxi Province.

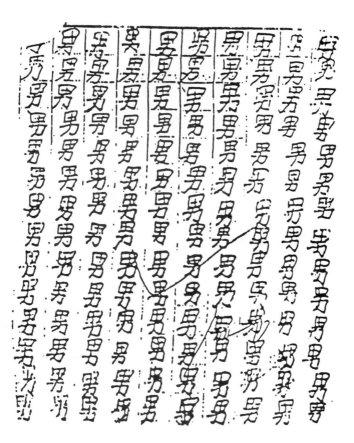

Sequence of Strokes

笔顺笔顺规则表

规 则 Name of Rule of Sequence	例字 Example	笔 顺 Actual Sequence of Strokes
先 横 后 竖	十	一 十
	下	一 丁 下
先 撇 后 捺	八	丿 八
	天	于 天
从 上 到 下 Up - Down	三	一 二 三
	尖	小 尖
从 左 到 右 Left - Right	地	扌 地
	你	亻 你
从 外 到 内 Outside - Inside	月	刀 月
	向	门 向
先 里 头 后 封 口	日	冂 月 日
	国	门 囯 国
先 中 间 后 两 边 Middle - Sides	小	丨 小 小
	水	丨 刀 水

**Workbook Practice Sheet for Learning Sequence of Strokes and
Position of Segments of Characters**

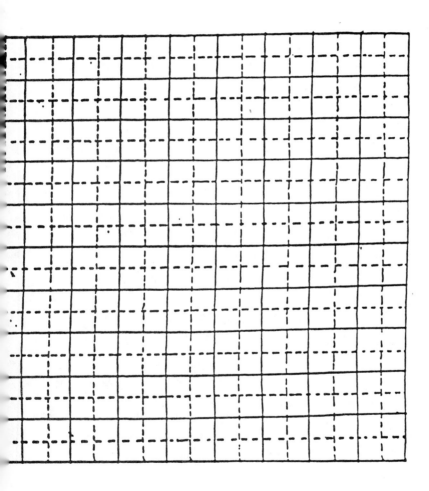

Note: The above figures have been reduced in size for publication.

ADVICE TO A DIALOGUE

JOURNALIST

Greta Nagel
Kathleen Kellerman

Many types of dialogue journals may be found in use across today's school campuses, from elementary to college level. The traditional and most common form of dialogue journal partnership is between teacher and student. Beyond that, classmates write to each other, sixth graders communicate with second graders, fifth graders befriend kindergarteners, students transmit messages between schools in different districts, states, or nations, and university students communicate with elementary school students.

The rewards of these journal partnerships are many. Through dialogue journaling, children have natural and meaningful opportunities for simultaneous reading and writing (Gambrell, 1985). It is motivating for partners to read words that address them as individuals, and it is helpful for them be exposed to the various perspectives of another person. Advocates of dialogue journals see benefits in the way they build upon natural conversation, provide real audiences, motivate accurate reading, promote social interaction, and enhance self-esteem as writers support one another (Bromley, 1989). Also, journals provide opportunities to go beyond written language that is used instrumentally, to get things done, to that which is used to reflect on the meaning and significance of activities when we use language to tell our stories (Britton,1975).

Unfortunately, these rewards are often offset by several interrelated difficulties when teachers dialogue with their own students. The hours required for a classroom teacher to respond to all her/his students' journals is burdensome. The amount of time to read and respond well to an individual entry varies with the grade level, but even a primary class set can easily take more than two hours. Teachers seem to counteract the time problem by writing brief, often simplistic, responses which cut short the opportunity to carry on true dialogue. For example, in one class of gifted fourth graders, the teacher's responses were seldom more than five or six words and focused upon exclamations such as "Wow!" and "That's great!"...affirmative, but hardly communicative.

Why We Did It

We were interested in developing a dialogue project where meaningful narratives could be written by both correspondents, for we saw the success enjoyed by peers in student-to-student projects. We designed our university/public school project and were encouraged by reports of improved writing enjoyed by students who participated in two reported adult-child buddy journal projects. We hoped to establish procedures that were appropriate, examine the written narrative texts, and analyze the outcomes for students at two different levels, fifth grade in elementary school and fifth-year, graduate-level teacher preparation.

Buddy journaling is a way for individuals to see life through the eyes of another person. It also provides opportunity for personal reflection. The ways in which buddies "listen" to one another can pave the way toward caring relations in the classrooms of the teacher-education participants. As the instructors of the two participating classes, we approached the project with a unified perspective that good projects in literacy education should meet multiple goals for our students: (a) development of skills (b) enhanced knowledge-base, (c) opportunity for self-expression, (d) chances to do problem-solving, (e) an arena to develop social ability, (f) a forum for emancipation, for breaking out of the narrow perspectives of one individual's groups (Nagel, 1992).

How We Did It

For two years, our respective students have written back and forth on a weekly basis in large college blue books. Initially, the college adults signed up for their respective buddies by choosing a name sight unseen from a school class list. During other quarters, the fifth graders would initiate name selection. The consensus among all teachers and students was to require weekly entries, but to establish no minimum length requirements, no weekly prompts, and no standard rubric. The fifth grade and the university writers maintained identical standards. The elementary students had all had a minimum of four months of independent journal writing prior to the project; none had ever written in a buddy journal. We teachers also maintained ongoing communication as buddies for each other.

The second ten-week set of journals was written between the same thirty-three fifth-graders and a new set of fifth-year university students during the new spring quarter. The procedures were identical to those of the first ten weeks except that all adults wrote to just one buddy and the end-of-journaling party was held on the university campus as a field trip for the fifth graders.

The third ten-week set of journals was written in the fall of the following school year. The writing proceeded according to the previous process with one additional approach that we devised. On five occasions, the university students were instructed to "embed" a different type of writing within the regular journal discourse. The five designated topics, spread over the eight writing opportunities, were: (a) an auto-biographical incident, (b) a descriptive narrative about a typical Saturday, (c) a biographical profile of a special friend or relative, (d) a description of my school, (e) a poem.

How Students Responded

Students, both young and old, enjoyed buddy journaling. When the distinctive journal bag arrived in either classroom, the students clamored, "Can we see our journals NOW?" All students shared weekly informal comments with their teachers and fellow students. Comments and reflections were collected informally over time and formally at the at the end of the university's quarter term. In the ninth week of each quarter, the fifth graders and the fifth-year college students responded to surveys about their participation in the project. The experience of meeting face-to-face was eagerly sought by students of both age groups. Fifth-grade and fifth-year students were equally enthusiastic about attending a joint event so that buddies could meet one another. On two occasions the university hosted a campus tour that included the Arabian horse barns along with a classroom luncheon visit. It had the dual advantage of having fifth graders experience the college campus and allow us instructors to view the future-teacher college students in their relations with the youngsters. During other quarters, an evening pizza party was held in the elementary classroom. It allowed the pre-service teachers to experience the public school environment.

Analyzing the Experience

We examined the written dialogue between fifth-grade students and their adult (ages 22-56) "buddies" who wrote as regular buddy journal partners. Our guiding research questions were intentionally broad: (a) What can university students in a teacher-certification class in Language Arts learn from active participation in dialogue journaling with students from a class that is diverse in socioeconomic status, ethnicity, and in English language acquisition levels? (b) What can fifth grade students learn from dialogue reading and writing with an adult who is preparing to be a teacher? (c) Will students' literacy skills be improved by the weekly written "conversations"?

As co-researchers, we analyzed: (a) 175 college blue books (16 pages each), (b) 90 fifth grade surveys (named) and 76 university surveys (named) for attributes of the journals and the journaling experience. Records included personal opinions about the success of the project and reasons for its value. We initially compared the adult answers to (c) 24 anonymous surveys that were administered to university students as part of a student-initiated research project (Reeves, 1993). We also compared notes, both literally and figuratively, through ongoing instructor-to-instructor journaling and face-to-face and telephone conversations.

We derived fourteen categories for careful page and line counts from the first and second journal sets: (a) Length of journals, (b) Topics of longest entries, (c) Episodes of modeling, (d) Lines that teach or explain How To, (e) Responses to questions, (f) Descriptions of school/school life, (g) Pets, (h) Family, (i) Sports, (j) Fads or specialized lingo, (k) Advice, (l) Personal, serious topics, (m) Disagreements or complaints, and (n) Compliments. Detailed counts were done on the second and third journal sets, meaning that data was drawn from the writings of two separate fifth grade classes and their buddies.

Findings in Response to Research Questions

The purpose of this paper is not to provide detailed statistics from our analyses. Rather, we hope that we can provide our readers with information that can guide them in developing their own buddy journal projects. We learned a great deal in response to our general questions.

(a) <u>What can university students learn</u>? In surveys, university students in a teacher-certification class indicated that they learned great varieties of information about how fifth graders view their worlds. Many college students commented that the journal experience enabled them to learn what it is like to be in fifth grade again.

One of many types of entries that characterized the dialogue journals involved the sharing values and lessons of life :

Dear Sandra,

> I think you should be proud of what you are. It doesn't matter what your color is, we are all the same. I sometimes think that I hate being dark or tan, but I am really proud of what my color of skin is....

Although we might expect a parent or a teacher to share such thoughts with a child, the words above are those of a fifth-grader to her twenty-five year old buddy, written in response to a future teacher, a middle-class Euro-American who had been bemoaning her "too-white" skin. The writer was a young Mexican-American girl who lives in the barrio of a small city.

In fact, the fifth-grade students spent more lines of narrative in instructing than did their college counterparts. Explaining what things are or how to do things seemed to come more naturally and frequently to the youngsters' writings. Another young writer impressed his older buddy with the following message:

> Hi,
>   God you san me the pacchr, I well sand a bedar picchar and I well gav your picchar and pellas gaw me oen dat I cod see your fas....
>   , senserele,

The young woman who had been writing this youngster was impressed by the weekly writing progress of a boy who had recently immigrated from the Middle East. She was delighted by the effort he displayed and she realized how, step by step, he was acquiring knowledge of English as a second language. They exchanged "better pictures."

(b) <u>What can fifth grade students learn</u>? Fifth grade students believed that they like their buddies very much, and were willing to correspond with a new buddy the next quarter. This willingness to continue journaling, from previously reluctant writers, provided a statement of literacy success in itself. Half of them reported that they learned specific things about their buddies and about college life, but not about any particular academic facts or concepts.

In reality, the teachers-to-be seldom "taught" the fifth graders. In non-embedded journals, only a few individuals told their buddies how to do anything. Most did not explain anything.

In non-embedded writings, topics usually followed patterns of small talk. Although there were no limitations on subject matter at either end, entries seldom went beyond patter (about hobbies, sports, pets, school, family, weekends, food, TV).

Students who were new to English could not understand the cursive writing of their buddies, nor could they comprehend many vocabulary words used by their older buddies.

Although adult students were involved in a literature-rich instructional program and were responding weekly to books in many positive ways, mention of books and poems was virtually nonexistent in non-embedded situations.

In several instances, adult topics that were beyond the parameters of home, school, or sports and were academic or business-oriented were incomprehensible to young buddies.

Adult students told about college as being a lot of work and having a pretty campus with lots of animals (there is a large school of agriculture). They did not discuss their reasons for being in college beyond wanting to be teachers, nor did they discuss any specific courses that they were taking. We discovered that they did not discuss liking school.

(c) Will students' literacy skills be improved by the weekly written "conversations"? Student writing varied in length and quality with the variety of topics discussed and buddy relationships. Also, students wrote longer entries in large-format journals than in journals that had small pages. We noticed that, unlike other reports of adult-child projects (Crowhurst,1992), there was no identifiable general trend toward greater fluency nor length in any individuals over the ten-week periods. That observation pointed us to implement the strategy of embedding that we used during the third ten weeks.

Assigned, embedded writings had a pronounced, positive impact upon length. However, the adults who wrote with apparent interest, as opposed to those few who said that they "had to write," evoked consistently longer responses in their young buddies. The narrative structure of the adult writings seemed to encourage similar narrative response in their young counterparts, and embedding appeared to increase narrative flow in surrounding adult journal entries. The longest entries for adults when the teacher-directed embedding had not yet been introduced were almost always their first entries, their introductions.

The longest entries for kids varied with interest in the topics. Themes that intrigued them beyond stories of self were summer, injuries, games. Successful partnerships wrote the most when they found common things that were of great interest to both buddies. Pets, families, and sports were the most favored themes.

Compliments were clearly related to the lengths of journals. The longest dozen journals in each academic quarter were written by top complimenters, both adult and student. On the other hand, the few adults who had buddies that they saw as "difficult" for any reason did not compliment their buddies, nor did they write any of the long journals.

The influences of modeling were clearly evident. Modeling helped determine greetings, closings, and—over time—correctness. It was also a two-way street. Tone, lingo, and standard spellings, punctuation, and capitalization were acquired by younger from older and by older from younger. Reflective writing encouraged reflective response.

Errors occurred in frequency with length of writings as well as with individuals' abilities. Longer entries had more spelling errors. Poor spellers misspelled words throughout their narratives.

Asking questions did not correlate with length. Asking multiple questions did not have a positive impact upon length nor quality of writing. Few fifth grade students retained narrative flow when they structured text in response to questions. On the other hand, stories modeled stories.

(d) Further findings included: Feelings of disagreement or discontent seldom arose, but when they did, they were in cross-gender buddy relations. Also, a few misunderstandings developed when adults did not have enough experiential context to understand such things as "Bloody Mary" games, certain playground games, or gang-style talk. Small irritations arose over situations such as, "I've asked you that question and you didn't answer me." Both young and old mentioned that it was an unusual experience to write to someone else at all. Several adults who thought they were having little success were, nevertheless, pleasantly surprised by the compliments of their fifth grader (and some parents) upon meeting their buddies at the end of the quarter. Connections between us instructors were enhanced by our writings as both a follow-up to the mechanics of accomplishing the project and as conversations. All students, both young and old, provided their buddies with more than journal entries. Stickers, drawings, jokes, snapshots, and/or cards were inserted into all journals.

Implications of our project

The success of buddy journaling was made clear by the excited anticipation of the journal reading in both the fifth-grade and fifth-year classes and by the unanimous approval of the project by both young and old students.

We believe that our findings support the following advice:

Advice to a Dialogue Journalist

1. Compliment your partner in genuine and specific ways. If your partner seems to be very different from you, or even "difficult," try even harder to be complimentary.
2. Embed personal life stories within your regular conversations.
3. Ask open-ended questions like "Has anything like this happened to you? What are your plans for the summer? What was your vacation like? What is your day at school like?"
4. Highlight your questions in such a way that you get your partner's attention; don't rattle on with a series of questions.
5. Make sure that your partner can understand your handwriting.
6. When your partner is new to English, do not use cursive writing, use simple vocabulary, add pictures to your writing.
7. Share the books and poems that you enjoy.
8. Teach your partner about something or how to do something.
9. Discuss your experiences at a level that your partner can understand.

10. If you don't understand something, ask. If your partner doesn't respond to your questions in a way that you understand, ask others for assistance.
11. Follow the tone of your buddy. For example, notice how your partner signs off.
12. Plan to meet your partner face-to-face, for what you think you know from the written word is not always the full reality.

Buddy journaling appears to be an effective way to help language arts programs reach goals of enhanced social ability, self-expression, problem-solving, and emancipation for BOTH fifth graders and fifth-year students. Dialogue helps all students to empathize with their younger or older counterparts as well as with individuals who are culturally different from them. *When appropriate strategies are used*, it is also an effective way to promote writing fluency and skill as well as help develop an enhanced knowledge-base.

With increased dialogue projects, correspondence may, indeed, be an art that won't get lost. Further teacher-preparation buddy projects can help inspire future teachers and students, promoting meaningful dialogue. In addition, such journals may save classroom teachers the tasks and time involved in writing to their students and provide all of the benefits of authentic writing. As we learned, buddies can certainly be university/public school partners. Many other writing relationships, such as between high school/elementary school, senior-citizen/middle school, within-class, or even high school/industrial buddies should have similar, positive outcomes if they follow our advice.

References

Britton, J. B., Burgess, T., Martin, N., McLeod, A., and Rosen, H. (1975). *The development of writing abilities*. London: Macmillan Education Ltd.

Bromley, K. D. (1989, November). "Buddy journals make the reading writing connection." *The Reading Teacher*, 43, pp. 122-129.

Crowhurst, M. (1992, April). "Some effects of corresponding with an older audience." *Language Arts*, 69, pp. 268-273.

Elbow, P. (1973). *Writing without teachers*. NY: Oxford University Press.

Gambrell, L. B. (1985). "Dialogue journals: Reading-writing interaction." *The Reading Teacher*, 38, pp. 512-515.

Goldman, L., Flood, J., and Lapp, D. (1992, November). *Journal writing between third and sixth grade students*. A paper presented at the annual meeting of The National Reading Conference, San Antonio, TX.

Heiden, D. E., and Schmitt, P. (1991). "Dialogue between sixth-graders and university students." *Reading Horizons*, 32, pp. 128-138.

Nagel, G. (1992). *"Good" groups: The search for social equity and instructional excellence through first-grade literacy groupings*. An unpublished dissertation. The Claremont Graduate School, Claremont, CA.

Reeves, J. (1993). *A look at correspondence between older and younger students*. An unpublished manuscript. California Polytechnic University, Pomona, CA.

ASIAN AND PACIFIC ISLAND STUDENTS: READING COMPREHENSION ASSESSMENT AND TEST ANXIETY

Linda M. Nolte
Velma A. Sablan

Introduction

Literacy groups in the United States have contended that one in five Americans are illiterate (Bok, 1990). Twenty percent of the population in the United States cannot read or comprehend what they read. In school systems, how one does on a reading comprehension portion of a standardized test, whether it be the Abbreviated Stanford Achievement Test (ASAT), the California Test of Basic Skills (CTBS), the Iowa Test of Basic Skills (ITBS), or any other device to ascertain students' ability to comprehend the written word, students' course placement is often determined by results on one of these instruments. Therefore, any instrument or teaching technique that can aid in helping students to become familiar with common rhetorical and syntactical devices and testwiseness may aid in the placement of students in more advanced courses. Consequently, when students are in courses that have higher expectations, they tend to rise to those expectations. When students are in more advanced courses and are exposed to higher level critical thinking skills, they have a better chance of staying in school and eventually getting accepted into a college or university instead of dropping out. Consequently, reading comprehension continues to be of grave concern for educators, parents, and students of today and those into the 21st century.

The educational achievement of linguistically diverse students is integrally tied to reading comprehension skills. Yet, many non-native English speakers "...may know more than they can communicate in English" (Wong, 1985, p. 9). Lave (1982) purports that in the real world people use procedures more complex than encountered or used in the classroom (taking tests to show competence). He further suggests that there may be a qualitatively different organization of metacognitive processes in different settings that are not formal test-taking situations. In other words, a test-type situation in the classroom or anywhere may not generate or indicate the true ability, potential, or knowledge of the test taker (Allen & Swearingen, 1991; Garcia, 1991). Consequently, linguistically diverse students' true academic potential may not be reflected and "...students often suffer underplacement in the academic program." Unfortunately for the classroom teacher, there is rarely any detailed feedback on which areas in reading comprehension students are having difficulty (Chavers & Locke, 1989). Garcia (1991) points out the shortcomings of most standardized reading tests, "It is difficult to know from such tests why any child does poorly" (p. 16). Are they missing questions with regard to inference, main idea, sequence, specific details? By having students self-report where they think their weaknesses lie, teachers will be able to target those areas so that their students will improve in reading comprehension.

Schema and Reading Comprehension

In mainstream American culture, linear processes are considered logical and important to understanding. Other cultures process or approach solving problems differently

(Garcia, 1991; Kaplan, 1966; Montano-Harmon, 1991; Szalay & Fisher, 1987). Hence, when trying to understand passages in English, students' background knowledge or schema is of utmost significance whether it be their linguistic, content, (Pehrsson, 1982; Devine, Carrell, & Eskey, 1988; McEachern, 1990) or cultural schema (Pearce, 1986; Pritchard, 1990).

A reader's linguistic schema aids in the ability to predict in a reading what will follow through the use of background knowledge or phonics and syntax. When readers cannot follow the arrangement of ideas in a text, they cannot successfully predict or generate ideas needed for seeing connections in order to comprehend text (Montano-Harmon, 1991).

Content schema refers to one's subject knowledge of material read while formal schema refers to the reader's familiarity with the narrative structure or organization of the material read (Kaplan, 1966). For students who do not learn English as their first language, background knowledge is important for developing reading comprehension skills (Chervenick, 1992).

Readers with different background or cultural schema may arrive at a different conclusion to a passage than the author intended (Steffensen, Joag-Dev, & Anderson, 1979; Pritchard, 1990). In addition, Luckham (1991) suggests negative attitudes towards reading lead to a lower vocabulary base which in turn affects reading comprehension.

Errors in reading comprehension may also be attributed to an inability to recognize specific words (Rupley & Willson, 1991), passage construction in tests and cultural bias (Chavers & Locke, 1989; Ford & Harris, 1994), a lack of testwiseness or lack of strategies to use when taking a reading comprehension test

(Herrera, 1991), prior schema interference, (Kinzer, 1982) or test anxiety (Williams, 1992).

Test Anxiety and Reading Comprehension

Definitions of test anxiety have been difficult for behavioral scientists because of the multifaceted nature of test anxiety and the lack of a multifaceted theoretical construct specific to test anxiety. Test anxiety is a special case of general anxiety and refers to phenomenological, psychological, and behavior responses that tend to occur in the face of possible failure (Sieber, 1980). Test anxiety is a phenomenon of both behavior and mind. Anxiousness is something that exists in the human mind and can have manifestations in human behavior.

Spielberger (1966) uses a state-trait model of anxiety where test stimuli leads to individualistic interpretation of that stimuli which in turn leads to an "A-state" which is described as reactions such as heightened arousal, vigilance, enthusiasm, fear, worry, confusion, illness, anger, or lowered self-esteem. Within this A-state, an individual may respond by becoming constructive, defensive, avoidant, or any combination of these. This response to the A-state is called cognitive reappraisal by Spielberger. What is interesting is that the engagement of any of these actions can produce either adaptive or maladaptive reactions.

Sieber, O'Neil, and Tobias (1977) have taken an operational approach to defining test anxiety. They include four specific approaches: (1) the phenomenology of anxiety which refers to an individual's awareness of the anxiety process, e.g., galvanic (intensely exciting electrical shock) skin response, pupil dilation systolic blood pressure, heart rate, increased breathing, and other observable bodily reactions, (3) performance of task, which refers to cognitive or behavioral measures taken during test taking, e.g., attention to task, memory, response time, and learning speed, (4) modifications of anxiety and its undeniable effects, which refers to studies which attempt to reduce anxiety through therapeutic change of social interaction, changes in perceptions, and changes in instructional settings.

Dweck and Wortman (1992) concluded from the literature on test anxiety that: (1) high test anxious subjects tend to perform more poorly on cognitive tasks, (2) they tend to report a greater incidence of task relevant thoughts during performance (most are self-deprecating in nature), (3) differences between high and low test anxious subjects increase when the test task is difficult or complex, and (4) the conditions under which a high test anxious subject performs enhances levels of apprehension and thereby decreases performance outcomes on a task.

Studies on test anxiety are extensive, but limited studies exist that observe cross-cultural differences among various ethnic groups. MacDougall and Corcoran (1989), in a study of test anxiety among graduate students tested in their home country of Taiwan, found no significant differences between Chinese and U.S. students on translations of anxiety measures. Nevertheless, they emphasize the need for cross-cultural studies for effective counseling of foreign students.

In a cross-cultural study of seventh and eighth graders, Guidan and Ludlow (1989) defined test anxiety as an unpleasant, emotional reaction to an evaluative situation. In a classroom, test anxiety is characterized by subjective feelings of tension, apprehension, uncertainty, and the activation or arousal of the autonomic nervous system which continues throughout the evaluative situation. In their study of test anxiety of four sample groups that compared black and white seventh- and eighth-graders from the U.S. (N=546) to eighth-grade students from Santiago, Chile (N=1,144), they found that significant main effects were obtained across culture, SES, and gender. U.S. students had lower levels of test anxiety than students in the Chilean culture. Higher SES groups reported less test anxiety than lower SES groups. Females reported higher levels of test anxiety than males. The only discrepancy to these findings was observed among high SES Chilean females where lower levels of test anxiety were reported compared to their male counterparts.

In their study of test anxiety to science examinations by fourth- and eighth-grade students, Payne, Smith, and Payne (1983) found no marked sex differences except for black fourth-grade students in comparing correlations between feelings about tests and science achievement test scores. Substantial race differences in magnitude of correlations for the total samples in both grades were evident. Differences were attributable to variations from one ethnic group to the other in motivational levels, study skills, inner self-efficacy, stress over time limits, and/or achievement motivation.

Test anxiety is definable, yet it lacks a cohesive multifaceted theoretical construct from which to test assumptions. There are cultural differences in the way various ethnic groups manifest test anxiety, and there are ethical dilemmas in defining and studying test anxiety. Research on test anxiety or by other psychological processes that are negatively regarded or deeply personal produces information about peoples' lives that must be carefully managed and monitored in all testing situations.

The present study was designed to address the following questions: (a) What is the Asian Pacific Island student's language base for reading and speaking? (b) What are the first and second languages used by the Asian Pacific Island student? (c) What are the areas of strength in identifying standardized reading comprehension constructs for Asian and Pacific Island students with regards to (1) confidence and (2) self-perceived knowledge? (d) What is the degree of test anxiety among secondary level Asian and Pacific Island students?

Method

<u>Subjects</u>

A total of 862 self-assessment reading questionnaires were filled out by seventh- through twelfth-grade students enrolled in seven different schools in San Diego County, California. The schools were located in areas that ranged from upper middle-class to inner-city. Ethnicity choices included African American, Asian American, Euro American, Filipino American, Latino American, Native American, Pacific Island American, and Other. Students were free to mark all that applied to them resulting in a total of 36 different ethnic combinations. Surveys with an ethnicity of Asian, Pacific Island, or Filipino were combined to profile the Asian Pacific Island students. Of the 862 students surveyed, 260 indicated total or partial ethnicity as Asian, Pacific Island, and/or Filipino. The ethnic breakdown of the Asian Pacific Island group is presented in Table 1.

Table 1
Ethnic Distribution of Asian Pacific Islander Sample Group

Ethnicity	*Percentage*
Asian	41.2
Filipino	39.6
Pacific Islander	4.2
Multi-ethnic Asian	7.7
Multi-ethnic Filipino	2.3
Multi-ethnic Pacific Islander	2.3
Multi-ethnic	2.7

Of the Asian-Pacific Island students, 118 were female, 134 were male, with eight (8) unidentified as to gender. Fifty-eight percent of the students indicated that they spoke English as their first language. Forty-eight percent of the students indicated that they spoke English as their second language. Eighty percent indicated that they preferred to speak English while 18.5 percent indicated that they preferred to speak a language other than English. Eighty-seven percent indicated that they preferred to read in English while nine percent indicated that they preferred to read in a language other than English. Four percent indicated no preference. Forty-six or 5.3 percent were in an identified ESL class, 27 or 3.1 percent were in twelfth-grade English classes, 261, or 61.3 percent were in ninth-grade English classes, and 528 or 61.3 percent were enrolled in seventh-grade English classes.

Instrument

For the purpose of analysis, the self-report reading questionnaire forms were divided into four sections. In section one, students could self-report: gender, ethnicity, language or preference for speaking and reading, and identification of first and second languages. In addition, the students identified their grade level and the English class in which they were enrolled. The second section provided an opportunity for students to self-assess their success with reading terms commonly found on reading comprehension tests (Green, 1988). Section three dealt with test anxiety and comfort level when taking tests. A 5-point Likert scale was used for sections two and three. The scale was structured as follows: 0 = no response, 1 = always, 2 = almost always, 3 = sometimes, 4 = almost never, and 5 = never.

Procedures

These assessments were completed in self-contained classrooms during the 1992-1993 and 1993-1994 school years and administered by the students' teachers. There was no time limit given to complete the survey. The data was then re-coded so that 1 and 2 responses were combined and 4 and 5 responses were combined. All comments were coded and entered on the Claremont Graduate School VAX mainframe and the San Diego State University VAX mainframe. The SPSS-x statistical software was used to analyze the data.

Results

Confidence in identifying semantical statements commonly used in reading comprehension questions varied. Tables 2 and 3 present student percentages for the semantic knowledge and confidence items. The students felt most confident in understanding the meaning of the word "setting" (88 percent), followed by 83 percent knowing what a topic sentence is, 81 percent knowing what the word "illustrates' means, 76 percent knowing what the word "theme" means, 68 percent knowing what the word "tone" means, 58 percent knowing what a passage is, 57 percent knowing what the word "motive" means, and 33 percent knowing what the word "infer" means.

Confidence in the ability to find certain concepts when reading also differed. Students identified finding the setting of a given passage the easiest to do (78 percent), followed by finding a topic sentence in a given passage (70 percent). The areas found most difficult to identify when reading were: inferring what an author intends (30 percent), inferring what an author feels (34 percent), figuring out what might have been stated in a missing paragraph (39 percent), identifying a topic sentence (41 percent), finding an author's purpose (49 percent), identifying tone (55 percent), and identifying an author's mood (57 percent). Three areas in which 58 percent of the students had confidence were in identifying what a passage illustrates, identifying an author's point of view, and identifying specific statements. Two areas of confidence were finding the main idea and identifying the best title at 61 percent. Finally, 62 percent felt that could figure out what a word meant from other words in a given passage.

Table 2
Results of Semantical Knowledge Items (N=26)

	ITEM	Always/ Almost Always	Sometimes	Almost Never/ Never	No Response
V8.	I know what a *passage* is.	**59%** n=154	29% n=76	12% n=30	
V11.	I know what the word *theme* means.	**76%** n=198	16% n=42	8% n=20	
V13.	I know what the word *illustrates* means.	**81%** n=210	10% n=27	8% n=21	1% n=2
V16.	I know what the word *motive* means.	**57%** n=147	25% n=64	19% n=49	
V18.	I know what a topic sentence is.	**83%** n=216	10% n=26	7% n=18	
V22.	I know what the word *infer* means.	33% n=85	31% n=81	**36%** n=93	.4% n=1
V28.	I know what the word *tone* means.	**68%** n=177	17% n=45	14% n=37	.4% n=1
V30.	I know what the word *setting* means.	**88%** n=229	7% n=17	5% n=13	.4% n=1

Percentages rounded to nearest tenth.   Highest percentages are in boldface.

It is interesting to note that in most areas students feel more confident with their perception of what a word means than in their ability to find an example when reading. For example, 76 percent felt they knew what the word "theme" meant while only 56 percent felt they could identify the theme of a passage. Eighty-one percent knew what the word "illustrates" meant, yet only 58 percent felt they could identify what a passage illustrated. Fifty-seven percent of the students surveyed felt they knew what the word "motive" meant, but only 41 percent could identify an author's motive. Eighty-three percent (83 percent) felt they knew what a topic sentence was, whereas only 70 percent felt they could find one while reading. Only 33 percent of the students surveyed identified that they knew what the word "infer" meant, while 34 percent felt they could infer what an author felt, and only 30 percent could identify what an author intended. Sixty-eight percent of the students indicated that they knew what the word "tone" meant, while only 55 percent felt they could identify the tone of a passage. Eight-eight percent (88 percent) of the students indicated that they knew what the word "setting" meant and 78 percent indicated that they could determine the setting of a given passage.

Table 3
Results of Confidence Items (N=260)

	ITEM	Always/ Almost Always	Sometimes	Almost Never/ Never	No Response
V9.	I can find the main idea of a given passage.	61% n=159	30% n=77	9% n=24	
V10.	I can identify the title that best expresses the ideas in a given passage.	61% n=159	29% n=75	10% n=25	
V12.	I can identify the theme of a given passage.	56% n=146	28% n=74	15% n=40	
V14.	I can identify what a passage illustrates.	58% n=150	28% n=74	13% n=35	.4% n=1
V15.	I can identify an author's purpose in a given passage.	49% n=127	35% n=91	16% n=42	

Table 3 cont.

ITEM		Always/ Almost Always	Sometimes	Almost Never/ Never	No Response
V17.	I can identify an author's motive in a given passage.	**41%** n=107	35% n=92	23% n=59	1% n=2
	I can find a topic sentence in a given passage.	**70%** n=181	21% n=54	10% n=25	
V20.	I am able to identify an author's point of view in a given passage.	**58%** n=150	32% n=82	10% n=27	
V22.	I am able to identify specific statements in a given passage that support the author's point of view.	**48%** n=124	36% n=93	16% n=41	1% n=2
V23.	I can infer from a passage what the author feels.	34% n=88	**34%** n=89	32% n=82	.4% n=1
V24.	I can infer from a passage what the author intends.	30% n=78	**37%** n=96	33% n=86	
V25.	I can infer what might have been stated in a missing paragraph.	**38%** n=101	37% n=95	23% n=61	1.2% n=3
V26.	I can figure out what a word means from other words in a given passage.	**62%** n=161	27% n=71	10% n=25	1.2% n=3
V27.	I can identify an author's mood in a given passage.	**57%** n=148	28% n=74	14% n=36	1% n=2
V29.	I can identify the tone of a given passage.	**55%** n=144	26% n=72	16% n=42	
V31.	I can identify the setting of a given passage.	**78%** n=202	16% n=41	6% n=16	1% n=2
V36.	I am a fast reader.	**43%** n=111	37% n=96	20% n=53	

Highest percentages are in boldface.
Percentages rounded to nearest tenth.

The majority of Asian and Pacific Island students reported that they were good test takers, and 33 percent sometimes perceived themselves as good test takers. Self-reports on anxiety had mixed results with less than half indicating they were anxious when taking an important test and 21 percent reporting that they did not get anxious when taking a test. The physiological reactions to test anxiety were particularly interesting. A total of 64 percent of the students indicated that they did not get stomach aches when taking an important test; a smaller percentage (48 percent) indicated that they did not get sweaty hands. This meant that more students tended to get the less overt reaction of sweaty hands as opposed to stomach aches in response to test anxiety. More than half of the students felt that they had enough time to finish a reading test. Confidence level was lower among students with 48 percent indicating that they felt confident about passing an important test. Table 4 gives the detailed breakdown in percentages of student responses.

Table 4
Results of Test Anxiety Items (N=260)

	ITEM	Always/ Almost Always	Sometimes	Almost Never/ Never	No Response
V32.	I am a good test taker.	54% n=140	33% n=85	13% n=35	
V33.	I get anxious when I have to take an important test.	43% n=113	35% n=92	21% n=54	.4% n=1
V34.	I get a stomach ache when I take an important test.	19% n=50	17% n=43	64% n=166	.4% n=1
V35.	My hands get sweaty when I take an important test.	27% n=71	25% n=65	48% n=124	
V37.	When taking a reading test, I have enough time to finish it.	54% n=140	34% n=88	12% n=31	.4% n=1
V38.	After taking an important test, I feel confident that I passed it.	48% n=124	38% n=99	13% n=35	1% n=2

Highest percentages are in boldface.
Percentages rounded to nearest tenth.

Discussion

To prepare students for the 21st century, it is imperative that educators understand why certain student populations do poorly on standardized reading comprehension tests. The purpose of this investigation was to glean insight from a test-taking population comprised of Asian Pacific Island students. First, this population's language base for reading and speaking was examined. Second, the identification of first and second languages used was identified. Third, student self-assessment of success with terms commonly found on reading comprehension tests in regards to confidence and self-perceived knowledge was analyzed. Fourth, possible test anxiety of Asian Pacific Island students and their comfort level when taking tests was investigated. Suggestions for future research are given.

Based on the results from eight items identified as semantical knowledge items, it appears that almost 70 percent of Asian and Pacific Island students are unsure of the meaning of terms such as tone (68 percent), passage (59 percent), author's motive (57 percent), and infer (33 percent). Many educators and test creators assume that students are not only familiar with these terms but that students know what they mean. But, are they taught? Do the students really understand them? According to this survey, the students do not believe that they know these terms.

The ability of this student population to identify certain items while taking a reading comprehension test is much lower. The areas of difficulty reported were inferencing (78+ percent), identifying an author's motive (59 percent), identifying specific statements that support an author's point of view (52 percent) identifying an author's purpose (52 percent), identifying a passage's tone (45 percent), identifying theme (44 percent), identifying author's mood (43 percent), identifying what a passage illustrates (42 percent), identifying an author's point of view (42 percent), identifying the best title (39 percent), finding the main idea (39 percent) and figuring out words in context (38 percent). Perhaps if this student population were taught how to identify the aforementioned areas and then given practice, results would be higher. Further, language arts curriculum need to address the issues of developing semantical background schema to aid in the students' abilities to not only feel confident that they can identify semantical terms used in standardized tests but confident in their knowledge of what these terms mean. Finally, as 48 percent of the Asian Pacific Island population in the survey indicated that English was spoken as a second language, future study needs to ascertain how much of the inability of the Asian and Pacific Island student to identify and understand semantical terminology is due to lack of linguistic schemata or language interference.

Strategies that may assist Asian Pacific Island students (or all other students for that matter) become more familiar with the process of taking a reading comprehension test are:

1. Practice cooperative group testing.
2. Have students explain to each other why a certain answer was chosen.
3. Encourage students to limit their response to only the words printed on the test; mention that they should not use outside information.
4. Administer practice tests orally. Asking questions about why the student choose a certain response may help identify any cultural logic discrepancies.
5. Allow students to use a dictionary during a standardized test to see what they can figure out when there is no constraint from time or lack of language awareness.

6. Make students aware of test format.

7. Encourage students to skip answers they do not know and come back to them later.

Based on the percentages that resulted from the six items on test anxiety, it appears that Asian and Pacific Island students feel that they are good test takers. They do not report any physiological responses to test anxiety, but many (46 percent) are anxious about test-taking. Time constraints do not appear to be a problem, and they tend to have confidence in passing an important test. The large number of students who reported feelings of anxiety when having to take a test (43 percent) conflicts with the results obtained from the remaining items. The question raised is whether these self-reports reflect a true profile of test anxiety among Asian and Pacific Islanders or more a reflection of cultural orientation or developmental growth state in adolescence. For an individual making the transition from childhood to adulthood, peer pressure and testing the boundaries of adult authority are constant struggles for the individual at the adolescent phase of development. Over confidence and apparent control over emotions even when they are not confident and in control are typical characteristics of this age group.

From the cultural perspective, Asian and Pacific Island students are frequently taught to hide or ignore feelings of stress and anxiety. Keeping calm and collected under stressful conditions is pervasive in Asian and Pacific Island cultures, so that thinking can remain sharp and clear in problem solving. Within this cultural group, feelings of stress and anxiety may then manifest themselves in other ways such as over-competitiveness, self-admonitions at failure, withdrawal, or depression.

Anxious behavior is generally considered negative and non-productive in Asian and Pacific cultures. Students tend to be taught to overcome feelings of anxiety by meditating and staying focused on the task at hand. Admitting to stomach aches and hand sweating when feeling anxious would be the equivalent to admitting failure or inability to do what is necessary to keep emotionally and mentally balanced. In other words, this admission would be interpreted as aggravating an already aggravating situation.

Some strategies that could be used to reduce test anxiety among Asian and Pacific Island students, or all other students for that matter, could be:

1. Do some intellectual warm ups before the test, e.g. word plays, guessing games, etc.

2. Do some relaxation exercises prior to testing, e.g. deep breathing, backward counting, memory games, etc.

3. Reassure students that tests are not the final word on their abilities, there are always opportunities to change and improve.

4. Diffuse the anxiety with humor, e.g. telling a joke or funny story about testing.

5. Do some simple whole body exercise routines prior to testing, e.g. deep breathing, arm stretches, shoulder rolls, etc.

6. Validate the students anxiety by recognizing it exists and providing opportunities for students to "talk out" the anxiety they are feeling.

7. Do a "psychological shedding" of the anxiety, such as going around the room with a bag or trash can, telling the students to take all the anxiety they are feeling and put it in the bag or throw it in the trash can. Then go through the motions of "throwing away" these feelings.

8. Do visualization exercises, e.g., have students close their eyes and imagine themselves doing well on the test. Have them "feel" themselves doing the best job they can do.

9. Be flexible about testing. Allow students to take the test at an earlier or later time so that they can choose the time of day that they feel most alert and ready to tackle the test.

10. Don't use tests. Be open to using alternative assessment strategies, e.g., portfolios, journals, writing, project pieces, and other authentic devices.

Further research in cross-cultural studies on the relationship between reading comprehension and test anxiety will require that survey items or interview questions are structured so that students can report on varying levels of anxiety and the methods they use to overcome these feelings. Developmentally appropriate and effective counseling procedures that are culturally sensitive to this group should be further explored.

References

Allen, D. D. & Swearingen, R. A. (1991, May). *Informal reading inventories: What are they really asking?* Paper presented at the Annual Meeting of the International Reading Association. (ERIC Document Reproduction No. ED 341 953.)

Bok, D. (1990, March). "Illiteracy knows no borders." *UN Chronicle*, p. 59.

Chavers, D. & Locke, P. (1989, April 4). *The effects of testing on Native Americans.* A paper commissioned by the National Commission of Testing and Public Policy. (ERIC Reproduction Document No. ED 336 445.)

Chervenick, E. C. (1992). *Schema theory: Teaching U.S. history to beginning amnesty students.* Unpublished thesis,

Biola University. (ERIC Reproduction Document No. 354 787.)

Devine, J., Carrell, P., & Eskey, D. (Eds.). (1988). *Interactive approaches to second language reading.* NY: Cambridge University Press.

Dweck, C. S. & Wortman, C. B. (1981). "Learned helplessness, anxiety and achievement motivation." In H. W. Krohne & L. Laux, (Eds.), *Achievement, stress, and anxiety.* London: Hemisphere Publishing Corp.

Ford, D. Y. & Garris III, J. J. (1994, July). "Promoting achievement among gifted black students: The efficacy of new definitions and identification practices." *Urban Education,* 29(2), pp. 202-229.

Garcia, G. E. (1991). *Factors influencing the English reading test performance of Spanish-speaking Hispanic children.* Technical Report No. 539. (ERIC Document Reproduction No. ED 334 563.)

Green, S. W. (Ed.). (1988). *Barron's how to prepare for the CBEST: California Basic Educational Skills Test.* CA: Barron's Educational Series, Inc.

Guidan, F. V. & Ludlow, L. H. (1989). "A cross-cultural study of test anxiety." *Journal of Cross-Cultural Psychology,* 20(2), pp. 178-189.

Herrera, K. R. (1991, June). *A research study to augment reading comprehension of gifted students through increased exposure to test-taking methods and strategies.* Unpublished Master's Practicum, Nova University.

Kaplan, R. B. (1966). "Cultural thought patterns in intercultural education." *Language Learning,* 16, pp. 1-20.

Kinzer, C. K. (1983, April). *Comprehension deficits from inability to shift schemata: Interference of existing knowledge on acquiring new knowledge from text.* Paper presented at the Annual Meeting of the American

Educational Research Association. (ERIC Document Reproduction No. ED 230 904.)

Lave, J. (1982). "A comparative approach to educational forms and learning processes." *Anthropology and Education Quarterly*, 13(2), pp. 181-187.

Luckham, M. R. (1991). *Increasing reading comprehension and positive attitudes toward reading through improving student vocabulary.* Unpublished Master's Thesis, Center for the Advancement of Education, Nova University. (ERIC Document Reproduction No. ED 335 665.)

MacDougall, M. A. & Corcoran, M. D. (1989). *The anxiety of Chinese students.* Paper presented at the Annual Meeting of the American Evaluation Association, San Francisco, CA. (ERIC Document Reproduction No. 318 308.)

MacEachern, W. R. (1990). *Supporting emergent literacy among young American Indian students.* (ERIC Document Reproduction No. ED 319 581.)

Montano-Harmon, M. R. (1991, May). "Discourse features of written Mexican Spanish: Current research in contrastive rhetoric and its implications." *Hispania*, 74(2), pp. 417-425.

Payne, B. D., Smith, J. E., & Payne, D. A. (1983). "Sex and ethnic difference in relationships of test anxiety to performance in science examinations by fourth- and eighth-grade students: Implications for valid interpretations of achievement test scores." *Educational and Psychological Measurement*, 43(1), pp. 267-270.

Pearce, D. L. (1986). "Improving reading comprehension of Indian students." In J. Reyhner, (Ed.), *Teaching the Indian child: A bilingual/multicultural approach*, pp. 70-81. (ERIC Document Reproduction No. ED 283 628.)

Pehrsson, R. S. (1982). *An investigation of comprehending during the process of silent reading: The Op-in procedure.* (ERIC Document Reproduction No. 236 573.)

Pritchard, R. (1990, Fall). "The effects of cultural schemata on reading processing strategies." *Reading Research Quarterly,* 25(4), pp. 273-293.

Rupley, W. H. & Willson, V. L. (1991, December). *Relationship of reading comprehension to components of word recognition: Support for developmental shifts.* Paper presented at the Annual Meeting of the National Reading Conference. (ERIC Document Reproduction No. ED 339 996.)

Seiber, J. E. (1980). "Defining test anxiety: Problems and approaches." In I. G. Sarason, (Ed.), *Test anxiety: Theory, research, and applications.* Hillsdale, NJ: Lawrence Erlbaum Associates, pp. 15-42.

Sieber, J. E., O'Neil, H. F., & Tobias, S. (1977). *Anxiety, learning and instruction.* Hillsdale, NY: Lawrence Erlbaum Associates.

Spielberger, C. D. (1966). "Theory and research on anxiety." In C. D. Spielberger, (Ed.), *Anxiety and behavior.* NY: Academic Press.

Steffensen, M., Joag-Dev, C., & Anderson, R. (1979). "A cross-cultural perspective on reading comprehension." *Reading Research Quarterly,* 15(1), pp. 19-29.

Szalay, L. B. & Fisher, G. H. (1987). "Communication overseas." In L. F. Luce & E. C. Smith, (Eds.), *Toward internationalism.* MA: Newbury House Publishers, p. 191.

Williams, J. E. (1992). *Effects of test anxiety and self-concept on performance across curricular areas.* Technical Report No. 143. (ERIC Document Reproduction No. 344 903.)

Wong, O. K. (1985). *Language assessment of Asian students: Problems and implications.* Technical Report No. 143. (ERIC Document Reproduction No. ED 253 563.)

INTERACTIVE STORYBOOK READING WITH YOUNG DEAF CHILDREN IN SCHOOL AND HOME SETTINGS

Linda Rowe
Bobbie M. Allen

The Commission on Education of the Deaf (1988) reported that "...the evidence clearly shows that the majority of deaf students have not been helped to achieve academically at a level equal to their hearing counterparts" (p. 17). The Commission also stated that reading ability has been highly correlated with prior English language knowledge and thus, many deaf children have had difficulty becoming proficient readers (p. 16). In general, the Commission attributed the reading difficulties of deaf children to deficits in experiential, cognitive, and linguistic variables.

Deaf children learn to communicate using a different symbol system, a visual spatial language, than hearing children who learn an auditory-oral language. Consequently, deaf children do not typically decode meaning from a sound-based alphabetic system as do hearing children. Ewoldt and Saulnier (1991) concluded that the deaf children ranging from 3 to 7 years did not go through the auditory decoding process. The children encoded the print directly to meaning. Some of the deaf children did not overtly demonstrate the association of the letter to sound. Other researchers have demonstrated that phonological mediation is not necessary for some readers to gain meaning directly from the print (Forster & Chambers, 1973; Vygotsky, 1978).

How deaf children learn to read and write has been an unsolved mystery for educators. Various traditional reading methodologies have been used which rely upon a student's understanding of the spoken English language and have so far yielded very little success.

According to Krashen (1985), if the linguistic input of the language role model is incomprehensible, the language output of the child will be severely delayed. It seems reasonable to assume that deaf children need to see a complete English model in order to become proficient users of the English language. Obviously, the printed word is one way for the deaf child to receive a complete and comprehensible English language model. Educators need to recognize and emphasize the importance of the printed word as one way of representing English as a complete and full language to deaf children.

On the other hand, American Sign Language (ASL) and the sign languages of the world have been recognized as languages in their own right. They are "...fully developed, autonomous, natural languages with grammars and art forms all their own" (Commission, 1988, p. 40). ASL should have the same status and respect as English in the classroom and should play an active part in the educational programs for the deaf. ASL, however, does not have a written component which is often a concern for many educators. Additionally, educators have been reluctant to use ASL in the classroom possibly because they are not skilled or fluent in the language. Researchers have reported that many teachers in the field are not skilled in any signed communication (Johnson, 1986; Kluwin, 1981; Marmor & Petitto,1979; Mather, 1987, 1989; Woodward & Allen, 1987).

Educators need to find ways of incorporating both languages, ASL and English, coactively in the classroom and in the home in order to facilitate language and literacy development of deaf children. Bilingual principles and strategies need to be further investigated as possible avenues for ASL and English to be used as the languages of instruction for deaf children.

How do young deaf children learn to read? Andrews and Mason (1984, 1986) asked this question and did a study about the emergent reading behaviors of deaf children between the ages of 5 and 8 years old. They identified 3 levels of change in word-reading development: (a) Level 1, the child knows about the printed word symbols, book handling, and attends to stories and labels pictures, (b) Level 2, the child recognizes words on food labels, cereal boxes and road signs, recognizes letters using finger spelling, and sequences and recalls stories, and (c) Level 3, the child begins to focus on the whole word and acquires a sight-word vocabulary rapidly; spelling and print knowledge increases as well as recitation of stories and sequencing abilities.

They concluded that "...children's communicative interactions about reading-related activities using finger spelling and manual signs with parents, teachers or peers act as precursors and possibly shape the reading-acquisition process to follow" (p. 28). They also concluded that deaf children and hearing children differ in one developmental aspect of reading. Hearing children can decode words through the graphophonemic structures of words whereas deaf children get meaning from the print without using a phonological system and use a system they can easily understand.

Padden and Le Master (1985) conducted a study of the acquisition of finger spelling in young deaf children. Finger spelling is a manual system consisting of various hand shapes for representing the alphabet. They found that children as young as 2 years old demonstrate an awareness of finger spelling. It should be noted that the first sign of deaf children can appear as young as 8 months old and three to four signed sequences can occur as early as 2 years old (Petitto, 1987). Children at this young age do not associate the hand shape of the letter to the corresponding written character. They noted that there are "... some similarities between those hypotheses that deaf children draw about finger spelling and those that hearing children draw about print..." (p. 171). Further research is needed in this area to determine the similarities, as well as how finger spelling contributes to the overall reading process for deaf children.

Williams (1994) conducted a case study of three profoundly deaf preschool children to investigate the children's emergent literacy development. Their ages ranged from 3:11 to 6:4 and all three children had hearing parents. She concluded that the "...Literacy activities and verbal interactions both at home and school were mutually reinforcing the children's language and literacy development" (p. 149). She reported that even though the children in the study appeared to have delays in language development, they demonstrated knowledge and understanding of literacy and participated in literacy events in appropriate ways.

Maxwell (1984) conducted a case study of a young deaf child's experiences with books. Alice's parents were deaf and were engaged in meaningful communicative interactions with her as soon as she was born using ASL, finger spelling, and speech. From his study, he concluded that Alice's sequential steps of story development paralleled that of hearing children's re-enactments of favorite storybooks (Sulzby, 1985). He also noted that Alice matched signs with illustrated signs presented in the book, "...then sign with sign illustration and printed word, then sign with sign illustration, print, and speech, as well as sign with sign illustration, printed word and finger spelling" (p. 121).

From the research, it appears that deaf children and hearing children develop language and literacy in similar ways. However, an obvious concern is the meaningful communicative interactions of deaf children with adults and their peers at an early age. One area that may facilitate communication between parents, teachers and deaf children, as well as develop language and literacy, is interactive picture book or storybook reading.

Interactive Storybook Reading in the Home and School

The interactive reading experience has been considered a contributing factor to early reading achievement (Durkin, 1966; Snow & Goldfield, 1982; Snow, 1983; Taylor, 1983; Teale, 1984). Kerr and Mason (1993) defined interactive story reading "...as the joint use of picture books to talk about the pictures, read the text, and discuss the story ideas" (p. 133). They described this approach as adults and children participating together in constructing and understanding a book. Through interactive story reading, children develop: (a) an awareness of written language, (b) a basic knowledge of storybook vocabulary and concepts and (c) the ability to identify letters and words associated with the story (p. 136).

Repeated reading sessions with the same book with children have also been documented. Snow and Goldfield (1982) concluded that the learning process of children in repeated interactive reading sessions becomes an avenue for children to learn to retell the story without prompts from the adult. Roser and Martinez (1985) found similar findings in that children tend to mimic the adult reader after repeated readings of a book.

Young deaf children of hearing parents (DCHP) often do not experience interactive storybook reading due to the lack of communication between the parents and the child. Hearing parents of deaf children are at a disadvantage. They have to cope with the deafness of their child and are also confronted with the task of learning a visual-spatial language, ASL, which is vastly different from an auditory-oral language, English.

Conversely, deaf parents of deaf children (DCDP) have natural communication with their children immediately and are not traumatized by their children's deafness. Deaf children with deaf parents have an enriched communicative environment which facilitates natural language development. Consequently, deaf parents with deaf children may have more opportunities to engage in successful interactive storybook readings. The strong language base of DCDP facilitates the acquisition of English and may be one of the factors contributing to their higher academic achievement than that of DCHP.

It is also crucial that educators learn how to incorporate ASL into the classroom to facilitate deaf children's understanding of English. Bilingual principles and strategies need to be examined as possible and viable avenues for identifying appropriate methods for using English and ASL as the languages of instruction for deaf children.

Strategies for developing more enriched interactions during interactive storybook readings using both English and ASL appear to be an important factor in developing language and literacy of deaf children. Mather (1987; 1989) investigated native versus non-native signers' strategies used in the classroom. She found that eye gaze as well as specific strategies and behaviors used by native signers created a rich and meaningful communicative environment.

Interactive storybook reading programs and workshops geared for parents and teachers to develop their sign language skills and interactive storybook reading strategies may provide an avenue for them to become more fluent signers and communicators.

It seems logical to conclude that deaf children and hearing children can develop similarly in language and literacy. However, early communication needs to be established in the home and at school for young deaf children. Interactive storybook readings may be one way that deaf children can have meaningful communicative interactions with their parents, teachers, and their peers. However, very specific strategies and techniques need to be incorporated especially during interactive storybook readings in order for deaf children to receive the maximum benefit.

Literacy Program

A model for presenting interactive storybook readings to a group of 18 to 42 month old deaf, hard-of-hearing, and hearing children was developed in a public school classroom. A parent component was also incorporated into the classroom program. The group ranged from 20 to 30 children depending on attendance.

The model was developed to present English and ASL in a manner that would demonstrate an equal status to both languages, give the children an opportunity to see each language used appropriately, as well as maintaining the attention and motivation of the group. It was clear that presenting English and ASL simultaneously would result in the loss of some of the linguistic features of both languages. In order to help the children, both hearing and deaf, to understand that ASL is a separate and distinct language from English, the following procedure was adopted.

For each page selected from the book, one teacher used oral English with facial expressions and voice inflections to give meaning and excitement to the story. The teacher that used English did not show the page to the children until she had finished her linguistic description of the picture or story narrative. After the English representation, the teacher using ASL would repeat a linguistic description of the same page using ASL. The ASL narrative was not an interpreted version of the English. The teacher made the story visually salient to the children using the best model of ASL possible. Strategies were employed that have been used by native signers to tell stories, such as miniature signing and signing directly on the page of the book (Mather, 1987, 1989). While the story was being signed by one teacher, the other teacher would hold the page facing the children. The children could see the picture, the signs and the printed text.

This team approach was an attempt to implement a model whereby the speakers of English and ASL could demonstrate that there were two separate and distinct languages involved in the telling of the story. The printed text also offered a way for the children to see English. The languages were therefore given equal status without either of them being compromised or modeled as an incomplete language.

During the team (ASL/English) approach to storytelling, the deaf children were observed engaging in various communication acts and behaviors. The deaf children were observed using voice inflections and mouth movements immediately following the English portions of the story. They also expressed portions of the story in ASL during or immediately following the presentation in ASL. When the children engaged in these types of behaviors, it appeared that they were demonstrating their awareness that the two languages were different and both were of equal value as there was no observed preference of one over the other.

For the most part, all the children appeared to be engaged and interested in the story. Of course, depending on the age of the child and possibly the story itself, some children were more interested than others. The teachers were accepting of the children's age appropriate behaviors and did not spend time redirecting their attention back to the story or the story tellers. Often other children who noticed their peers not watching the story would direct their "unattending friend" towards the story.

The more the children were exposed to stories using this approach, the more they tended to pay attention and enjoy them. If the teachers were especially dramatic and expressive, they were able to hold the children's attention and raise their curiosity for longer periods of time, During other times of the day, the children selected the familiar books as one of their preferred activities and attempted to retell the stories to their deaf and hearing peers as well as the adults.

After the story, time was built into the schedule to allow the children to share books. This was probably the most interesting part of the process. Initially there were only one or two copies of the book that had been read to the children available to share. There was a wide selection of other age appropriate books available for the children to select. However the children did not seem satisfied with the other books The majority of the children wanted to "read" and share the book that the teachers had just presented during story time. Following this observation a

classroom set of books was purchased so all the children could
share the same story at the same time.

   The teachers were amazed and intrigued with the ways the
interactions among the children changed when they all had a
copy of the same book to share. The children were observed
using a variety of social functions, as well as frequently using
inquiry, response, and request behaviors. During book sharing
with the same book, the children's communication dyads were
observed to be more frequent and sustained.

   The classroom literacy program was so successful it was
extended into the home. An identical set of books was
purchased for the children to have at home to be shared with
their parents and family. With some assistance from the
classroom teachers as part of the home visit component of the
program, the parents were able to to tell the same stories at home
to their children. The results were impressive. One mother
reported her daughter refused to go to bed until her daddy read
her a story. This was a family who spoke only Spanish and had
minimal signing skills. Despite what could be considered
serious barriers to communication, the child's interest in books
seemingly generated by the story telling time at school resulted
in an opportunity for communication at home. After *The Three
Little Pigs* had been read in class, another child, upon seeing a
small hole in the wall of the kitchen at home, signed to his
mother to indicate that the wolf had blown the hole in the wall.

   It would appear that this story telling model is a way to
facilitate the development of English and ASL, as well as an
interest in books with young deaf, hard-of-hearing, and hearing
children. Early exposure to a variety of experiences with written
language activities, interactive storybook readings, and
meaningful communicative interactions in the home and school

settings will promote and enhance language and literacy development in young deaf children. It is hopeful that deaf children who are engaged in these types of activities early on will reap the benefit of increased academic achievement that is commensurate with their hearing counterparts and thus become literate and successful adults in our society.

References

Andrews, J. F., and Mason, J. M. (1984). *How do young deaf children learn to read? A proposed model of deaf children's emergent reading behaviors.* (Technical Report No. 329). Champaign, IL: University of Illinois at Urbana Champaign.

Andrews, J. F., and Mason, J. M. (1986). "Childhood deafness and the acquisition of print concepts." In D. B. Yaden & S. Templeton (Eds.), *Metalinguistic awareness and beginning literacy.* Portsmouth, NH: Heinemann.

Andrews, J. F., and Taylor, N.E. (1987). "From sign to print: A case study of picture book "reading" between mother and child," *Sign Language Studies*, 56, pp. 261-274.

Commission on Education of the Deaf. (February, 1988). *Toward equality: Education of the deaf* (A Report to the President and the Congress of the United States. Washington, DC: U.S. Government Printing Office.

Durkin, D. (1966). *Children who read early.* NY: Teachers College Press.

Ewoldt, C., and Saulnier, K. (1991). *Engaging in literacy: A longitudinal study with three to seven year old deaf participants.* Final report for the Gallaudet Research Institute, Center for Studies in Education and Human Development. Washington, DC: Gallaudet University.

Forster, K., and Chambers, S. (1973). "Lexical and naming time," *Journal of Verbal Learning and Verbal Behavior*, 12, pp. 627-635.

Johnson, R. C. (1986). "How teachers communicate with deaf students," *Perspectives for Teachers of the Hearing Impaired*, 4(5), pp. 9-11.

Kerr, B. M., and Mason, J. M. (1993). "Awakening literacy through interactive story reading." In Lehr, F. & Osborn, J. (Eds.), *Reading, language and literacy*, pp. 133-148.

Kluwin, T. (1981). "A rationale for modifying classroom signing systems," *Sign Language Studies*, 31, pp. 179-187.

Krashen, S. D. (1985). *The input hypothesis: Issues and implications*. NY: Longman.

Marmor, G., and Pettito, L. (1979). "Simultaneous communication in the classroom: How well is grammar represented?" *Sign Language Studies*, 23, pp. 99-136.

Mather, S. (1987). "Eye gaze and communication in a deaf classroom," *Sign Language Studies*, 54, pp. 11-30.

———. (1989). "Visually oriented strategies with deaf preschool children." In C. Lucas (Ed.), *The sociolinguistics of the deaf community*, pp. 165-187. San Diego, CA: Academic Press.

Maxwell, M. (1984). "A deaf child's natural development of literacy," *Sign Language Studies*, 44, pp. 191-224.

Padden, C. A., and Le Master, B. (1985). An alphabet on hand: The acquisition of finger spelling in deaf children," *Sign Language Studies*, 47, pp. 161-172.

Roser, N., and Martinez, M. (1985). "Roles adults play in preschoolers' response to literature," *Language Arts*, 62, pp. 485-490.

Snow, C. (1983). "Literacy and language: Relationships during the preschool years." *Harvard Educational Review*, 53, pp. 165-189.

Snow, C. E., and Goldfield, B. A. (1982). "Building stories: The emergence of information structures from conversation." In D. Tannen (Ed.), *Analyzing the discourse: Text and talk*. Washington, DC: Georgetown University Press.

Sulzby, E. (1985). "Children's emergent reading of favorite storybooks: A developmental study," *Reading Research Quarterly*, 20, pp. 458-481.

Taylor, D. (1983). *Family literacy: Young children learning to read and write.* Portsmouth, NH: Heinemann Educational Books.

Teale, W. H. (1984). "Reading to young children: Its significance in literacy development." In H. Goelman, A. Oberg, & F. Smith (Eds.). *Awakening to literacy.* Exeter, NH: Heinemann Educational.

Vygotsky, L. S. (1978). *Mind in society.* Cambridge, MA: Harvard University Press.

Williams, C. L. (1994). "The language and literacy worlds of three profoundly deaf preschool children," *Reading Research Quarterly*, 29(2), pp. 125-155.

Woodward, J., and Allen, T. (1987). "Classroom use of ASL by classroom teachers," *Sign Language Studies*, 54, pp. 1-187.

THE POWER OF THEORY: CASE STUDIES OF ADULT NEW READERS, WRITERS, AND SPEAKERS OF ENGLISH

La Vergne Rosow

ESL and native-English adult learners can acquire language forms and vocabulary naturally along with content, especially when they understand what causes literacy and language acquisition. This essay highlights some of the content of a presentation made to educators at the 1995 Claremont Reading Conference, "Towards Multiple Perspectives on Literacy." During my presentation, a case was made for teaching theory to adult learners.

Adult poor- and non-readers who have to survive in a literate world are daily faced with reinforcement of their early lessons... lessons that they were unable to read and write...lessons they learned very well. The adults in this study had learned early on that teachers are on earth to judge and gate-keep, and that school is a place to be humiliated. (For background on literacy problems in the U.S. see Kozol, 1985.) This article is about some of those who discovered the truth about the literacy process and how to apply it to their own lives. The truth, in this case, is simply the theory that empowering teachers apply, either overtly or subconsciously, day-by-day. Of course, the adults you'll meet here had not encountered such teachers, nor had they a clue that the power of theory was something they themselves could wield on behalf of themselves and their children.

More than just an overview of their individual cases, though, I will show you how I conveyed the keys to empowerment—methods and materials of literacy and language arts—*in process* and how some learners, in turn, applied that new knowledge to other aspects of their lives. The strategies shown here are ones I have used in workplace education with classes ranging from twelve to twenty, in community college English as a second language and reading classes of forty and fifty students—some with 17 different native languages, and individual tutoring in literacy volunteer work. Not all of the adults showcased here were my personal students, though I did have direct contact with all of them. Some were students in an experimental adult literacy program I founded through the California Literacy Campaign, tutored by volunteers (volunteers who, by the way, acquired graduate level reading and research skills over time). For confidentiality, all participant names have been changed.

Also, there are two reading lists. One is a very short annotated bibliography of readings I've found effective in language and literacy work with adults. Some of it is clearly adult literature to be read aloud to the students; some is officially categorized as *children's literature*. (I have a bit of a problem with that category as a significant percentage of my personal leisure reading collection is in it. At what age are we supposed to stop loving inspiring pictures and beautiful colors?) The other is the list of readings that professionals from ESL and reading will want to own. They make up the formal reference list at the end. But I hasten to add that the "professional" literature is frequently very interesting to the adult learner, so it was with great reluctance that I kept these lists separate. If you are inclined to combine them, bravo!

In italics throughout this essay are theoretical terms and concepts that I use frequently when working with adult learners.

It is by no means a comprehensive collection, just very high frequency. I've found that teaching the adult the actual language of theory empowers the learner to think in theoretical terms and to feel more secure when speaking with other adults about literacy, for example when discussing a child's performance with a teacher. Certainly I don't teach The Vocabulary List, but I do introduce the actual terms right along with the concept. Different terms are addressed in different cases here for the sake of brevity, but nearly every case applied every theoretical concept sooner or later.

Danny - Applies Key Words and Language Experience

Key words and *language experience* are present in some form or other throughout my work with new readers and with adults just learning English. Danny, a high school graduate who was nearing his fiftieth birthday when we met, was quite intimidated about speaking to large groups. And records revealed he had moved backwards from reading at the first grade level to below first while working with the twelve teachers he'd had over several years in a volunteer literacy program. Though he drove both surface streets and freeways for a living, he claimed difficulty even reading a STOP sign.

During our initial session, I introduced him to a litany of theoretical concepts and sources, including the work of Septima Clark who used *key words* among Blacks needing to pass a literacy test to vote during the pre-civil rights era of the Deep South; Sylvia Ashton Warner who used "organic" words of the Maori kindergartners, making extraordinary gains with these previously thought "unteachable" wild children of New Zealand; and Paulo Freire, the lawyer turned literacy advocate, as he taught the peasants of Brazil to do reading and writing heretofore thought beyond their capabilities. I asked him if he would like to try *key words* in our work. Seemed worth a try, he thought, and after five minutes of mind wrenching, he finally came up with one word that was very important to him—*freeway*. After that, he spoke into my tape recorder nonstop for about 15 minutes on this topic that was straight from his heart. Please allow that the fact that the teacher was not enamored with freeways was beside the point; this was about learner interest. I took the tape home and transcribed half a page of text, creating a learner-centered piece of reading material. The following session, I showed the passage to Danny and explained the term *language experience*. Then I asked him to see how many of the words he could identify. Haltingly at first, and then with enthusiasm and embellishment, he conquered the entire text. That is to say, when confronted with text that made sense to him, that was based on his *background knowledge*, that used his vocabulary and turn of phrase, Danny was able to read...for the first time in his entire life. *Learner-centered* literacy activities work very quickly. "Oh, that's tricky," he said, "this program really works!" (Rosow, 1995, pp 143-182).

In this way, Danny began to write extensive essays. From the beginning his work had a strong, Danny voice. (For more on author's voice, see Graves, 1994, pp. 81-82.) While reading an essay aloud, he would discover changes he needed to make for clarity, depending on the audience he needed to reach. Danny's sense of audience needs emerged almost without instruction. Sometimes following questions I asked, sometimes on his own, he evolved into the process of editing and finally published his work in the literacy program newsletter. The essays were designed to teach tutors about the *affective filter*, the editing process, and the importance of *learner-centered* instruction. Understanding the theory behind his learning and knowing that he was using the same language as that used by professionals in the field, Danny knew how to discuss reading and writing education. During the last month of our tutoring time, the previously crowd-shy Danny eagerly read his essay "The Tutor Who Had a Loud Mouth" aloud to an audience of prospective literacy volunteers.

Miguel and Maria - Find Text Through TPR

In an entry level community college ESL class, Miguel and Maria were enrolled to accumulate their legally mandated amnesty education hours. Suffice it to say that they were externally motivated to be in class. Neither had prior schooling. And neither was literate in Spanish or English. The act of writing was so strange to Miguel that he broke down in tears as he tried to force marks from the side of a pencil with a broken lead. Though they were quite literally lost in the required programmed workbook activities—they were unable to even recreate the needed letters and words I wrote on the chalk board—they did respond to one of the most fundamental of literacy devices... *language experience.* (This is very simple when the teacher speaks the same language as the learner. He just gets the learner to tell about an experience as he, the teacher, acts as secretary. Not so when teacher and student speak different languages.)

Because Maria was expecting a child and because both adults were concerned about the language to use at the hospital which would include family information, I began by extracting information about their other children. I knew from prior class discussions (via hand signs, pantomime, and drawings on the chalk board) about doctors and hospitals that some of their children had been born in the United States. That gave me the foundation I needed to jump into more *TPR (total physical response)* activities that made sense to the couple (Krashen, 1985 and 1988; for an excellent overview of the whole language philosophy read Goodman, 1986). I acted out "baby" and "holding," then "emergency" and "children." In this way we collected a variety of words that were meaning-filled for them. And a *learner-centered* story emerged.

As I printed each letter by hand I repeated the word and talked about the process of putting words on a page—leaving a space between the letters, using a capital for the name of a child, putting a period at the end of a sentence. (Just after the text was done, I was afraid I'd dumped a lot of meaningless information on them when what they needed was elementary vocabulary. Later I realized it had been fine.) At the end of each sentence I would read the entire sentence, for example, "Jose is six years old." Then I would ask Maria and Miguel, "Is this true? Is this what you want?" Little by little they began to understand that the text was coming from them and that they were in charge of its development. It was like seeing empowerment bloom before my eyes as the jumble of letters and English words they'd faced hopelessly in class began to hold messages that they would use when they spoke of their most valued asset, their family. For a page and a half I wrote simple sentences, often repeating the same vocabulary from the text before. Suffice it to say, this was not an attempt at fine literature—yet. But it was an introduction to literacy that Miguel and Maria could own. Nothing less learner-centered would have made the same impact in so short a time.

When the story was complete, I *read* the entire piece to *them*, again checking to see if they agreed by using gestures to illustrate things like the heights of the children as I spoke. I'm often asked if I pointed to the words as I read. No. That would be fostering poor word-by-word reading habits that could slow reading and impede comprehension forever. But, non-readers may have no idea where to focus at first, especially in a page of solid text with no pictures. So I did keep one finger at the start of the line I was reading, guiding the new readers down the page, while allowing the entire text to show. This full-page exposure permitted the opportunity for skipping and regressing that would emerge as they took on independent reading.

By the time the writing and rereadings were complete, I'd actually repeated every word many times—but not as a drill and practice—just as a normal way of explaining what I was writing and what I had written. It was practice *in process*. Then I asked if either of them wanted to try reading some of it. Incredibly, Maria was able to read through the entire text, almost flawlessly. Miguel had more difficulty, but could speed up as he hit the names of his children, getting an almost visible boost of courage to move ahead through more unknown. He read nearly all the text, let out an extended sigh and sobbed. In just one sitting, these two adults had moved from pre-literate to new reader status. We made photocopies of the story so that they would have meaning-filled text to read at home and to use as a model for their writing.

This particular process was only possible because other students were engaged in cooperative learning activities and attendance was low that day. Had the entire class been present, it would have been impossible. I have met with students outside of class to negotiate such successes, but admittedly there is a limit to the energy a human has—even a teacher human—and there is a limit to number of hours there are in a day. And such a breakthrough is not enough to launch adults into the world of literacy. There must be a stockpile of quality reading materials in the classroom, so that the teacher can assist in selections, and to support home reading.

But just the presence of books with good pictures will not provide the sound-symbol relationships good readers make in their heads. It takes a lot of quality *input* before quality output can be expected. Adults who don't know what good reading sounds like need *to be read to*—a lot. Even though I was an adjunct instructor, meeting in different classrooms from week to week (Yes! Finding the classroom was a major challenge for these students all semester long), I did manage to cart in a small leisure reading library, had fifteen minutes of SSR (sustained silent reading) at the start of each class, and read at least one story aloud to the class each time we met. I also had a collection of beautifully dramatized books and tapes to loan out. For couples like Miguel and Maria, these were the only ways to get them acquainted with quality literature for their children. In the process of teaching them language, I also introduced the value of *reading* to their children and the importance of letting children see their parents reading for fun at home. This theoretical foundation gives the adult learner an "excuse" to handle those well illustrated, easy-to-read books that may have always seemed untouchable.

Classroom reading practice need not be assigned. Indeed, given the best of circumstances, there will be so much opportunity to read, an assignment to do it all would seem overwhelming. Because many of the students were in the amnesty program (facing deportation if citizenship was not acquired within a fixed time frame), I brought in and put up posters with the *Pledge of Allegiance* and other citizenship-related material to create a *print-rich environment*. Little by little, words like "indivisible" began to appear in student journals.

Jonathan - Who Critically Analyzed SSR

To three high school youths I introduced the little teaching papers I'd developed on the *self-fulfilling prophesy* and the

affective filter. We had extensive discussions and all confirmed
that these issues applied to their own experiences.[1] And of
particular interest was the early childhood profile of the adult
non-reader I had identified. Among other things, it showed two
100 per cents: One-hundred percent of the time, the adult
non-reader had no memory of being read to for pleasure—in the
preschool years or early school years. And one-hundred per cent
of the time there was a history of child abuse—either profound
neglect, physical violence, or both (though often it was reported
as appropriate discipline, rather than abuse) (Rosow, 1988, pp.
15-16). A group interpretation of *language experience* was also
a process I employed there. But here I want to focus on
authentic texts and *sustained silent reading (SSR).* Authentic text
is the only way to introduce powerful writing style, and SSR is
key to every literacy and language teaching situation I can think
of.

One of the young participants was Jonathan, who hated
reading and all things relating to literacy when we met. He'd
been in special education since the fourth grade, but had never
learned that reading can be a pleasurable experience. Over time,
he proved a perceptive observer, forming theoretically grounded
explanations for his criticisms of the disempowering practices in
the schools he'd attended.

During a discussion of *readability levels*, Jonathan was
intrigued to see how uninteresting chopped up reading materials
became when they were allegedly "simplified" for the students in
his special education category. Though logically he agreed that
smaller words and shorter sentences should have been easier to
read, he soon was able to move beyond that simplistic view of
language into an understanding of how *background knowledge*
and *reader interest* would impact comprehension and reading
speed. He also discovered that, consistent with the claims I'd

made, writing style is very much aligned with the kind of reading one does. And as he read—or as I read to him—his own cognizance of written language developed.

After comparing *authentic* and *simplified* (aka *adapted*) texts, Jonathan was quite literally appalled to discover that the same information delivered in straight-forward language was not only easier to comprehend, but that he could even enjoy previously dreaded history when it was couched in rich, anecdotal material. The detail-intensive treats, traditionally reserved for the advanced students actually seemed worthwhile. Indeed, during our few months together, Jonathan became a history buff, specifically focusing on war, and requiring the history magazines available in the open stacks of his local public library.

Jonathan and his group cronies were at once interested and skeptical in the research studies I presented on sustained silent reading. Even when I showed them the charts in Krashen's little book *Insights and Inquiries* (1985), it was hard for this jaded trio to buy the notion that in schools where SSR is appropriately handled for over six months all students—high and low achievers—have increased standardized test scores—across the curriculum. (Though all of my teaching encourages questioning and fosters learner responsibility for truth-seeking, working with these three teenage lads caused me to hone my own oral defense skills more than any formal education experience had ever done.) So, I set out to clearly outline exactly what is supposed to be good about SSR:

> The reader decides what is interesting and what is not. If it is interesting, comprehension will increase, even when the vocabulary is challenging or when new concepts are

introduced. If it is boring, the reader is expected to put the book down and try something else.

The reader may read material that is very easy. When that happens, the reader will encounter more vocabulary and syntax and will increase his or her reading speed.

The reader is at liberty to read a lot of unrelated things, acquiring broad knowledge to support further reading.

The reader may read intensively about one subject, causing vocabulary to develop at very high levels.

The reader may revisit books or stories already enjoyed, experiencing the relaxed sense of story without stress.

The reader is in charge of the reading. That links intellectual power and decision-making with the act of using text for one's own purposes.

There is no testing or other accountability. This removes external stress typically associated with school related reading.

There are no external rewards. No grades, no points, no prizes. That makes the joy of reading the pay-off and encourages life-long literacy, as opposed to something like a job you will leave when the pay-checks stop.

After this discussion they seemed to think I might be on to something.

We talked about the value of having lots of good books at various levels handy, so that everyone in the class could find something worthwhile and easy to read during the school's emerging SSR program. That also made sense to them. Yet the need for the student to be explicitly informed about pedagogical motives came to light when Jonathan realized that his former English teacher had not been lazy, but had been applying good theory, when she required no book reports on SSR "work." He suddenly understood that testing would have made it impossible for him to do the extensive rereading he required for the comprehension that would lead to enjoyment. Just having time to look at a book of choice, to move ahead, skip around, or back up, was, in itself empowering. Too, having a girlfriend (who happened to be a good student) to discuss the science fiction book she'd given him also supported comprehension. Then Jonathan's school changed principals, enabling him to observe the impact that theoretical understanding has on the practice of something as fundamental as SSR. The new principal wanted "accountability." As a result, the students were suddenly forced to document their SSR readings and report on content in ways that made the previously relaxed language arts activity suddenly become part of the regimented curriculum. Jonathan remarked that this new principal just didn't understand what SSR was about. He was right. Though he was not in a position to change the philosophy of the educators at the helm of his school, he was no longer inclined to think that his failure to adapt to misused activities meant that he was suddenly unable to learn. The power of theory let Jonathan analyze the situation around him and evaluate the process from an informed perspective. Jonathan began to make plans for continuing the education he had previously longed to end. And rather than dropping out of high school, Jonathan was contemplating college.

Ella - Connected Soccer and Literacy

Ella was a very shy young woman who had been prevented
from attending high school in the U.S. because she could not
obtain her school records from Samoa. (She could have attended
as a freshman, beginning the high school experience over, but as
a physically large teen-aged woman, moving back three years in
school promised more emotional and academic trauma than she
could face. Not attending at all proved easier.) As a result, she
had worked as a sitter for family children and then got a low
level factory job where the language requirements were minimal.
She had access to no Austronesian literature and was unable to
read the available English, so the early literacy skills she had
acquired slowly eroded. Though she might have come into the
adult literacy program for help at any time, her motivation by the
time we met was to help her little girl who was about to enter
school. During her first interview, she related personal
anecdotes to the *affective filter* concept and to the *self-fulfilling
prophesy* referenced above. She also indicated a strong interest
in soccer. Based on information from our intake interview, her
tutor established a learner-centered program that included
reading from Frank Smith's *Insult to Intelligence* (1988)
(particularly the chapter on dealing with schools), reading story
books, and writing letters to other parents active in her child's
soccer team. Ella was told why they were doing what they were
doing and she was invited to suggest change in her curriculum,
which she often did. Within just a few months, Ella had become
the preschooler soccer coach, was writing powerful
philosophical letters to parents about the spirit of the game, was
reading full popular novels to herself and quality children's
literature to her daughter, and she had given an emotionally-
charged, very well informed lecture to new tutors about how to
support the writing process for adult learners.

Theory and Issues In Summary

The theoretical notions, methods, and materials discussed here outline the high-frequency issues common to all of my adult learners, both ESL and new readers. At the conference, I passed out copies of theoretical terms which we then discussed within the context of adult learner case studies. Now, I want to recap those issues and address some concerns voiced by colleagues and other professionals.

Print-rich environment - The most literal translation of this term I've ever seen was in Milt Goldman's reading classroom at Hamilton High School in Los Angeles. Even the ceilings are covered with posters of pop stars and record albums. Everywhere you look, there is something to read, usually supported by pictures. Scott Joplin's album has his picture and his name—every time you look his way. That kind of meaning-filled reading practice causes literacy to develop even when no thought to reading is being stated. Students long graduated, return to visit Goldman. The price of admission: a poster. Out-of-pocket expense is often a problem for new—and not so new—teachers. Even for teachers on a minimal budget who must traipse from classroom to classroom, free publisher's posters collected at conferences allow some such environment dressing to occur. Student-made slogans and posters are another way of getting high-interest, low cost colorful print on the walls. There has been the argument that print-rich environments distract students who are often more interested in what's on the walls than what's in their workbooks. My suggestion is to put the desired content into impossible-to-ignore, irresistibly beautiful posters and allow daydreams to occur at will.

TPR or total physical response - Total physical response is just that. The student points to the word "throw" in a story, for example, and the teacher picks up a piece of paper, wads it up and throws it across the room. At the beginner levels, there's nothing more powerful. Though it is somewhat distracting during SSR, students come to expect it. I generally write the word or phrase in question on the board for the benefit of those who may wonder at what the current activity represents. Yes, TPR takes a lot of energy. On the other hand, it also relieves the teacher of the high cost of aerobic exercise classes.

In process - In process may be viewed as the philosophical opposite of in isolation. As referenced here, theory is taught to the adult learner, not as a separate set of terms, but in the context of the reading and writing process. You learn language experience, for example, by hearing the story of how Warner applied it in New Zealand and then by having your tutor write down your language experience story. The opposite approach might be to be given a vocabulary list, isolated from meaningful experience, and a test on same at the end of the week. Never having experienced the theory applied, you might well fail the test...and so would your teacher.

Affective filter - This is a wall of feelings that rises when the learner is under stress. When the filter is high, new information cannot get into the brain. There has been some argument that people can perform very well under stress. The fact that an adrenaline rush manages to facilitate success in incidents so unusual that they are remarked upon does not indicate that a state of constant fear would help anyone learn better. When people are relaxed, comfortable, well-rested and well-fed, they are better prepared to learn.

Self-fulfilling prophesy - Once a learner understands that he or she cannot do something, such as read, speak, write, or draw well, the learner will make that prophesy come true.[2] Teacher expectations program student achievement.

Key words - Key words are key to the LEARNER. They are thought up by the learner for use in literacy activities. Traditionally and as described here, they come from one learner and are documented by one teacher. In my workplace classes, though, I have taken words brainstormed by the entire class as I wrote them on the whiteboard and have allowed the entire class to decide which word or words would be key to a group generated story. This can work when a common background, such as familiarity with a defective machine, creates great interest on the part of all participants.

Language experience/learner-centered - Language experience employs the language and the experience of the LEARNER to create text that is meaningful to the learner. The case of Miguel and Maria shows how one story can come from two people with a common concern. And for the three high school students I wrote stories based on experiences they had collectively reported. From a purist sense, this has been challenged as not actually being "true" language experience. Alas, it simply empowered the learners by giving them *learner-centered*, meaningful text to read.

Background knowledge - This is everything the learner already knows and understands about a subject. It includes ideas, vocabulary, and experiences. Teachers can build the background knowledge of an entire class by providing group experiences...like a field trip to a used book store.

Learner interest - Learner interest is essential to concentration. If the learner is forced to "study" uninteresting topics during the time she is supposed to be learning to love reading, she will learn that reading for her is very uninteresting. Such lessons had been learned quite thoroughly quite early among the adults discussed here.

   Sustained silent reading (SSR) - SSR is detailed extensively in Jonathan's case.

   Reading to adults/input and output - Before a person knows what good reading is supposed to sound like, she must hear it. Before a person knows what great written language looks like, he must either see it or hear it. (Written and spoken language are not identical.) So, *reading to* adult new literates and new English speakers is an essential source of quality input. It would be a waste of time and would teach learners that they are inept to require output before input has been provided. Jonathan, Danny and Ella were all three victims of this premature call for output, this test, masqueraded as teaching.

   Readability levels - There are a variety of scales, prescriptions and formulas out to evaluate the difficulty of text. Generally speaking, they look primarily at sentence length and word size. Some attempt to consider the various parts of speech or other grammatical issues that can be quickly identified by a machine. They do have a value in that they give us a fast way of evaluating text that is already written, especially if we want to sort readings into categories for learners we have never met. I particularly like using the Fry Readability Scale, because Fry has devised a little slide-rule to facilitate the demystification process. Once students understand what makes up grade levels, they are much less intimidated by them (Rosow, 1995, pp. 212-213). Unfortunately, these formulas are sometimes applied to text that has already been written for the purpose of manipulating or "simplifying" it. Not looking at the background knowledge or interest of the reader, the text manipulators presume to know which words are easy and which will be too difficult for readers they've never met. They may substitute little words for big ones. They may also chop compound and complex sentences into a strip of simple ones. Such text tampering can damage the style, rhythm, and flow of written language. It may also impede comprehension. (See authentic text below.)

Authentic text vs. simplified or adapted text - Authentic is the term used to describe the text as first published under the author's signature. Simplified or adapted is not the author's language, though frequently the new reader is unaware of this, because publishers promote the name of the quality author, even when the text is significantly altered by an unknown who may have followed a grade level prescription or formula without understanding the impact they were making on their unmet readers. Once, when I had two community college classes of the same level back to back, I was able to conduct research on Steinbeck in *simplified* and *authentic* forms. Though the language of the Steinbeck novel should have been way over these students' heads, I discovered that not only did they retain detail from the *authentic* work, they also applied vocabulary met only once...in the powerful style known only to readers of the real thing. The students exposed to the same story line, but in simplified text watered down to reportedly ostensibly meet the lower level student needs, remembered little and showed no vocabulary acquisition as a result of the reading. A group of high school honors students in one of my tutor education classes suddenly came to the realization that they had been given adapted texts under the guise of the real thing, presumably in the name of censorship...to protect them from offensive scenes and language. When the students ferreted out the real literature and saw what they had missed, they were appalled. One young man realized that his dislike of a famous author was caused by the fact that the meat and guts of the original work had been siphoned out of his school books, leaving him to study lifeless husks. Tampered with texts should be so labeled.

Quite a different matter are *retellings* of folktales, myths and legends, so old the source is unknown or original language unintelligible. In such cases, the named reteller may well be using the language that comes naturally to propel the story. Such is the case when Ann McGovern retells the three-thousand-year-old Aesop fables. (Incidentally, McGovern's easy-to-follow language has been very helpful to me in both adult and family programs.) And sometimes a folktale's lesson is delivered in a contemporary format, causing such significant changes that "retelling" is not an accurate description. An example of that is Phoebe Gilman's *adaptation* of a Jewish folktale she calls *Something from Nothing*. In this case, Gilman has taken a story that shows up under different titles in different books and given it her own title, engaged her own characters, and delivered anew an inspirational old values lesson. Though the original tale was probably created in an oral tradition, and though collections of folktales may tell the entire tale in half a page of text, Gilman's interpretation provides a book filled with detailed illustrations and just a few lines of text per page, perfect for the adult learner who may first hear the teacher read it aloud in class, may then read it silently during SSR, and then may take the book home to read to children, confident that the pictures will facilitate recall of words that would still be impossible to read in isolation.

Translations, too, can hold close to the spirit and flow of the original text, while making it accessible to speakers of other languages. In such cases, the idea is to stay tied to the meanings created by the original author, not to escape high-intensity language.

It has been suggested that adult new readers and ESL students need simplified texts because they can't understand the more complex forms of language. First, let me suggest that when the teacher is *reading to* the students, the teacher can stop along the way, supplementing meaning with anecdotes and gestures. In this setting, he can employ much higher level text to introduce students to elegant turns of phrase and less common vocabulary. Well-written language is decidedly more colorful than simple, conversational English. That clearly calls for authentic text. Secondly, for the student's own reading, there is a wealth of authentic text available that introduces language use in the context of culture and anecdotes necessary for deeper understanding of many classical readings. To skip over the literature foundation that successful literacy students have had years to acquire is to create a void in the adult learner's experience...and impede comprehension and appreciation of many readings forever after. Perhaps every bit as important as those two arguments, however, is the need to believe in the native intelligence of our adult learners. If they could speak a language, any language, by the age of five, they have enough brain power to do ANYTHING. We must be very cautious not to limit their opportunities for development by limiting access to authentic language.

Literature for adults and children's literature - If the child enjoys hearing the adventures of Sherlock Holmes read aloud by her mother, does that make Sir Arthur Conan Doyle's work children's literature? If I put Byrd Baylor's *The Table Where Rich People Sit* (1994) among my favorite leisure readings, does it become adult fare? And what about Aesop fables? They were first told as political satires for adult ears. Sometimes they appear in huge collections in tiny print. At other times they appear as a single story filling a beautifully illustrated volume. At what point do we assign them to one age group and remove them from another? I think never. Quality literature speaks for itself. Adults who lack a pleasure reading habit are inclined to parrot stereotypical notions about books in an effort to cover up their unfamiliarity. They fear the unknown. Part of our charge as empowering educators is to help ease their discomfort around beautiful books by sharing them.

The more adult learners know about what causes literacy and language to develop, why certain methods are being tried, and how good readers and writers employ literacy, the easier it will be for them to take charge of their own learning. If our mission is to create teacher-independent, life-long learners, we must transfer our knowledge...all of it...to the people who will continue to be in charge of the learning process--the learners themselves.

A Few Good Readings for Adult SSR, Leisure Reading, and Other Study
Compiled by La Vergne Rosow

The 1995 Claremont Reading Conference attendees received reading lists that included books available for sale through the conference and many that were shared during my session. In lieu of the hands-on opportunities afforded by Mrs. Nelson's Book Store and my personal collection, annotations are provided.

The middle passage, illustrated by Tom Feelings, New York, NY: Dial Books, scheduled for release in November of 1995. This is to be a picture history book, one that belongs in every American's library.

Life doesn't frighten me, poem by Maya Angelou, paintings by Jean-Michel Basquiat, Stewart, Tabori & Chang: New York, poem copyright 1978, illustration copyright 1993. It looks like a simple picture book. It is a chilling social statement.

Fables for our time and famous poems. Illustrated. James Thurber. (1983). New York, NY: Harper & Row. These little two- and three-page fables poke fun at everything and everyone sacred to Americans. They are great short reads.

Love you forever. Robert Munsch. (1986). Toronto: Annick, 1986, 28 pages. This is the cycle of life, a book worth reading and having and giving away.

Something from nothing, adapted from a Jewish folktale by Phoebe Gilman. (1992). New York, NY: Scholastic. Here is an old folk tale with a powerful message, delivered with marvelous illustrations.

Aesop's fables, retold by Ann McGovern. Illustrations by A. J. McClaskey. (1963). New York, NY: Scholastic.

Uncle Jed's barbershop. Margaree King Mitchell. Illustrated by James Ransome. (1993). New York, NY: Scholastic. picture book. Already an old man, Uncle Jed loses his life savings, starts over, and over again. This is an inspiring success story.

Babushka Baaba Yaga. Patricia Polacco. (1993). New York, NY: Philomel. Suspicion, intolerance, bigotry, and fear keep the unusual looking old Baaba Yaga from the loving relationships she needs. . . until she devises a cover-up.

The paper bag princess. Robert Munsch. (1980). Toronto: Annick. Here is a spoof on all past helpless female fairy tales with a grown-up solution.

The ever-living tree, the life and times of a coast redwood.
Linda Vieira. Illustrations by Christopher Canyon. (1994).
New York, NY: Walker. Here is world history, ancient history,
prehistory and basic science all in one very beautiful book.

A river ran wild. Lynne Cherry. (1992). San Diego, CA: A
Gulliver Breen Book, Harcourt Brace Jovanovich. The true
story of a river used, abused, killed off and revitalized gives a
huge chunk of American history in this tale of ecology.

The great kapok tree: A tale of the Amazon Rain Forest. Lynne
Cherry. (1990). San Diego, CA: A Gulliver Breen Book,
Harcourt Brace Jovanovich. Here is a must have for every
library.

Rainforest secrets. Written and illustrated by Arthur Dorros.
(1990). New York, NY: Scholastic. The secrets this book holds
need to be learned quickly, while there's still time.

The giving tree. Shel Silverstein. (1961). New York, NY:
Harper & Row. Here is the cycle of life and the life of a tree
with wonderful language and a good story.

Animalia. Graeme Base. (1986). New York, NY: Harry N.
Abrams. This alphabet book is so beautiful it can be a wedding
gift. It is also good for birthdays, rainy days, and days when
nothing else is going on. Jerry Pallotta has written a series of
well illustrated, well researched, scientific alphabet books on
enough topics to keep an ESL class going all semester.
Following are just three.

The extinct alphabet book. Jerry Pallotta. Illustrated by Ralph
Masiello. (1993). Watertown, MA: Charlesbridge.

The flower alphabet book. Jerry Pallotta. Illustrated by Leslie Evans. (1988). Watertown, MA: Charlesbridge.

The frog alphabet book. Jerry Pallotta. Illustrated by Frank Mazzola. (1990). Watertown, MA: Charlesbridge.

Ruth Heller also has a series of scientific books, all written in whimsical rhyme with soundly documented data. Here are three.

How to hide an octopus, and other sea creatures. Ruth Heller. (1992). New York, NY: Grosset & Dunlap.

Plants that never ever bloom. Ruth Heller. (1984). New York, NY: Grosset & Dunlap.

The reason for a flower. Ruth Heller. (1983). New York, NY: Grosset & Dunlap.

The man who planted trees. Jean Giono, Wood Engravings by Michael McCurdy, afterword by Norma Goodrich. (1985). Chelsea, Vermont: Chelsea Green. 53 pages. This fictional story makes the power of the individual seem quite probable.

A fire in my hands, a book of poems. Gary Soto. (1990). New York, NY: Scholastic. This book of poems gives the background of each, making it an excellent writing discussion book.

The table where rich people sit. Byrd Baylor, pictures by Peter Parnall. (1994). New York, NY: Macmillan. I've introduced this book to every educator I can corner. All have become richer for it.

Stellaluna. Janell Cannon. (1993). New York, NY: Scholastic. The humorous side of differences that create social strife for bat Stellaluna and her adoptive bird family.

Smoky night. Eve Bunting. Illustrated by David Diaz. (1994). San Diego, CA: Harcourt Brace & Company. Caldecott Winner. The Los Angeles riots are brought very close to home through sensitive text and bold, new, adventurous collage illustrations.

Days of courage: The Little Rock story. Richard Kelso, Alex Haley, General Editor. Illustrations by Mel Williges. (1993). New York, NY: Steck-Vaughn, 89 pages. Racism and bigotry are key elements in this part of the U.S. story. Though it is about America, this book fosters discussion of racism worldwide.

Four against the odds, the struggle to save our environment. Stephen Krensky. (1992). New York, NY: Scholastic. Four true stories about individuals who made a difference.

History's big mistakes. Adam Bowett. Illustrated by Chris Mould. (1994). London: Belitha Press. 32 oversized pages. Yes, big mistakes, all over the world. One such story is about the Dust Bowl, further detailed in the following book.

Children of the Dust Bowl, the true story of the school at Weedpatch Camp. Jerry Stanley. Illustrated with historic photographs. (1992). New York, NY: Crown Publishers. The disasters of nature and economics drove the Oakies from their Oklahoma farms to the unfriendly doorsteps of California.

Explorers who got lost. Diane Snsevere Dreher. Illustrated by Ed Renfro. (1992). New York, NY: Tom Doherty Associates.

135 pages. Here is true history at its funniest worst, well illustrated and easy to read.

The hundred dresses. Eleanor Estes. Illustrated by Louis Slobodkin. (1973). New York, NY: Scholastic. 79 pages. Mercilessly ridiculed for her poverty, the child in this story claims to have a hundred dresses in her closet. In a way, she does.

How many days to America? A Thanksgiving story. Eve Bunting. Illustrated by Beth Peck. (1988). New York, NY: Clarion. Regardless of the country of origin, my ESL students have related to this beautifully illustrated book about a family running in terror from oppression.

All those secrets of the world. Jane Yolen. Illustrated by Leslie Baker. (1991). Canada and United States of America: Little Brown & Company (Canada) Limited. This little war book is chilling and thought-provoking.

The war began at supper: Letters to Miss Loria. Patrician Reilly Giff. Illustrated by Betsy Lewin. (1991). New York, NY: Delacorte Press. Here a series of letters to a beloved student teacher reflect many social issues in plain, everyday English.

America at war! Battles that turned the tide. Brian Black. (1992). Scholastic Inc.: New York. Name the war and it is here, waiting to support the study of American history through conflict around the globe.

The Guinness book of records, 1995 edition. Peter Matthews, Editor. New York, NY: Bantam Books. There's something of interest for everyone in this storehouse of short passages.

Unfortunately, the paperback version has relatively small print, but, after all, the two-inch-thick book talks about practically everything in the world.

The world almanac and book of facts 1995. Editor Robert Famighetti. Mahwah, NJ: Funk & Wagnalls. 975 pages. What you didn't find in Guinness, you'll find here.

Reference Books for Adult Literacy and ESL

The following five Ruth Heller books are part of my classroom library reference collection, defense against the question about what a certain part of speech represents. With only a few words per incredibly beautifully illustrated page, Heller moves the reader from simple to complex forms of grammar and syntax. For those who can get past the pictures, the content is forthright and easy to understand. Heller doesn't hold back on language, so after reading Heller, my students' writing commonly shows up with ten dollar words like "explode" and "opulent." This series is still in process. I highly recommend all you can find.

Kites sail high, A book about verbs. Ruth Heller. (1988). New York, NY: Sandcastle, Grosset & Dunlap. This book is so beautiful and easy to understand that company administrators who did very badly in elementary English classes want it for their personal collections.

Merry-go-round, A book about nouns. Ruth Heller. (1990). New York, NY: Grosset & Dunlap.

A cache of jewels, and other collective nouns. Ruth Heller. (1987). New York, NY: Grosset & Dunlap.

Many luscious lollipops, A book about adjectives. Ruth Heller. (1989). New York, NY: Grosset & Dunlap.

Up, up and away, A book about adverbs. Ruth Heller. (1991). New York, NY: Grosset & Dunlap.

Longman dictionary of American english, a dictionary for learners of English, White Plains, New York, NY: Longman, 1983. Written for use by English as a second language (ESL) and English as a foreign language learners, this clearly written book also works well for the adult new reader.

A dictionary of American idioms, second edition. Adam Makkai, New York, NY: Barron's, 1987, 398 pages. OR
Barron's handbook of commonly used American idioms. Adam Makkai, Maxine T. Boatner, and John E. Gates. Hauppauge, New York, NY: Barron's Educational Series, 1984, 296 pages.

The complete rhyming dictionary, edited by Clement Wood, revised by Ronald Bogus. New York, NY: Dell, 1991, 705 pages. Students who are intrigued by dictionary study are easily diverted when more meaningful lists of words are provided. This book assists in the creation of text.

A writer's guide to transitional words and expressions, Fourth Printing, Victor C. Pellegrino, P.O. Box 967, Wailuku, Maui, Hawaii, USA 96793-0967: Maui Arthoughts Company, 1991. This very thin book is so good I keep a copy next to my computer. Its two pages full of alternatives to "said" are worth the space.

The star-spangled banner, illustrated by Peter Spier, New York, NY: Dell, 1992. This is the National Anthem illustrated and more.

For more selections, see *La Vergne Rosow's Annotated List of Good Books*, (Rosow, 1995, pp 277-297) and Rosow, L. (in press 1996). *Light 'n Lively Reads for ESL, Adult and Teen Readers*. Englewood, CO: Libraries Unlimited.

Footnotes

1. The full texts of these papers are found in appendices A and B in L. Rosow, (1995). *In Forsaken Hands: How Theory Empowers Literacy Learners*. Portsmouth, NH: Heinemann. I invite you to just read them to your students as written. Actually, as these little papers apply the concepts of the original studies—which focussed on children—to the adult learner, they bring the concepts close to home.

2. For more information on this see Appendix B and Chapter Seven, pages 183-224, in L. Rosow, above.

References

Byrd B. (1994). *The table where rich people sit*. Pictures by Peter Parnall. NY: Macmillan.

Gilman, P. (1992). *Something from nothing*, adapted from a Jewish folktale by Phoebe Gilman. NY: Scholastic.

Goodman, K. (1986). *What's whole in whole language*. Portsmouth, NH: Heinemann.

Graves, D. (1994). *A fresh look at writing*. Portsmouth, NH: Heinemann.

Kozol, J. (1985). *Illiterate America*. NY: Anchor Press/Doubleday.

Krashen, S. (1988). *Fundamentals of language education*. Torrance, CA: Laredo.

_____. (1985). *Inquiries and insights*. Hayward, CA: Alemany.

McGovern, A. (1963). *Aesop's fables*. Retold by Ann
    McGovern. Illustrations by A. J. McClaskey. NY:
    Scholastic.
Rosow, L. (1988). "Adult illiterates offer unexpected cues into
    the reading process." *Journal of Reading*, 11, pp. 20-24.
_____. (1995). *In forsaken hands: How theory empowers
    literacy learners* (working title). Portsmouth, NH:
    Heinemann.
_____. (in press 1996). *Light 'n lively reads for ESL, adult and
    teen readers*. Englewood, CO: Libraries Unlimited.
Smith, F. (1988). *Insult to intelligence: The bureaucratic
    invasion of American schools*. Portsmouth, NH:
    Heinemann.

NOTES ON CONTRIBUTORS

BOBBIE M. ALLEN has been in the field of deafness for 15 years. Her teaching experiences are broad ranging from early childhood to university levels. She has been a faculty member at San Diego State University involved in the preparation of teachers of the deaf. She is currently a faculty member in the Teacher Education Program at the University of California, San Diego and a joint doctoral candidate at San Diego State University and The Claremont Graduate School. Publications, presentations and research areas have been primarily related to nonverbal and verbal communication acts observed in young deaf children and the development of an on-going ASL proficiency evaluation for teacher education programs.

CAROLYN ANGUS is Associate Director of the George G. Stone Center for Children's Books, The Claremont Graduate School. She is a frequent presenter of workshops for teachers, librarians, and parents. Her special areas of interest are children's literature and elementary science.

MARY A. BARR is Director of the California Learning Record Project whose purpose is to develop an alternative method of assessing student learning for public accountability. Prior to this commitment she was Executive Director of the California Literature Project.

MARTIN BONSANGUE is Associate Professor of Mathematics at California State University Fullerton where his research focuses on ways to improve student achievement in mathematics.

NANCY BONSANGUE is a speech/language pathologist with the Placentia-Yorba Linda Unified School District in California.

GARRETT DUNCAN writes extensively in the areas of language and literacy, adolescent development, and critical educational theory.

DIANNE JOHNSON-FEELINGS earned an M.A. in Afro-American Studies and a Ph.D. in American Studies at Yale University. She now lives in her home state with her husband, artist Tom Feelings, and their daughter Niani. Johnson-Feelings teaches children's literature, young adult literature, and African American literature at the University of South Carolina. She is author of *Telling Tales: The Pedagogy and Promise of African American Literature for Youth* and *Presenting Laurence Yep.* She is the editor of *The Best of the Brownies' Book.*

KATHLEEN KELLERMAN teaches fifth grade at Acadia Elementary School in Fullerton, California. She earned a B.A. in Psychology from Stanford University and an M.A. in Education from The Claremont Graduate School.

GRETA NAGEL is Director of the "Teach for Pomona" Alternative Certification, California State Polytechnic University, Pomona. Prior to this she was a public school teacher, principal, and university teacher educator. She holds a Ph.D. degree from The Claremont Graduate School and San Diego State University.

LINDA NOLTE is a joint doctoral student at The Claremont Graduate School and San Diego State University. She is currently employed by the San Diego Unified School District as a Secondary English/ESL teacher.

JOHN REGAN, HAO KE-QI, HUANG PING-AN, ZHANG, WEI-JIANG, YANG CHANG-QING. The authors are members of one of the research groups of associates established between Claremont and Chinese educational institutions. In these research groups, individual educators join together in furthering understanding of educational issues and problems through comparison with a contrastive culture. The principal investigator in the research reported here, John Regan, is professor at The Claremont Graduate School in the Center for Educational Studies. Hao Ke-Qi is professor, and Huang Ping-An instructor, at the distinguished Xi'an Jiaotong (Communications) University in Xi'an, the ancient capital of China. Yang Chang-Qing is president, and Zhang Wei-Jiang English Department dean of Wei'nan Teachers' College, adjoining the site of the ancient terra cotta army excavations, and to become the center of a first community college network.

LA VERGNE ROSOW is currently Literacy Coordinator of JobLink, a national workplace literacy project funded by the U.S. Department of Education. Rosow has an M.A. in instructional media and photography, an M.S. in teaching English to speakers of other languages, and an Ed.D. in intercultural education with an emphasis in language teaching and literacy.

LINDA ROWE has taught very young deaf children and their parents since 1962. She has also been a faculty member at the University of Southern California and San Diego State University where she has been involved in the preparation of teachers of the deaf. She has presented at a variety of conferences, workshops, and symposia during the past 30 years. She has published, primarily on the subject of the development of speech in deaf speakers. She is currently on the faculty of Lafayette Elementary School in San Diego, California where she teaches in the Early Childhood Coenrollment Program.

VELMA SABLAN is Associate Professor of Education at the University of Guam and an authority on cognitive and language

development. A specialist in multicultural education, her
research about the language development and thinking strategies
of children in Micronesia has achieved widespread recognition.

JANET SHARP is an Assistant Professor of Math Education, in
the Department of Curriculum and Instruction at Iowa State
University. She has worked with elementary and secondary
math teachers around the country.

LIL THOMPSON, teacher extraordinaire, former Infant School
Headmistress and the subject of two BBC films on teaching, has
been inspiring participants in the Claremont Reading Conference
for the past twenty-two years. Her message has been consistent:
language in all its forms requires a kind of creative teaching
which encourages children to see it, not as much an end in itself,
but as a means for thinking and communicating.

JANET WONG received the 1994 Southern California Society
of Children's Book Writers and Illustrators award in poetry for
Good Luck Gold and Other Poems. She has also written *The
Trip Back Home* about her return to Korea at age five. Ms.
Wong holds a B.A. degree in History from UCLA and a J.D.
degree from Yale Law School. She was a practicing attorney in
Southern California for several years before beginning her
writing career.

DATE DUE

GAYLORD | | | PRINTED IN U.S.A.